READING THE RIGHT BOOKS

A Guide for the Intelligent Conservative

© 2007 by The Heritage Foundation
214 Massachusetts Avenue, NE
Washington, DC 20002-4999
202.546.4400 ● *heritage.org*

Printed in the United States of America

ISBN: 978-0-89195-127-8
Photo credit: Spencer Anderson

READING THE RIGHT BOOKS

A Guide for the Intelligent Conservative

Edited by Lee Edwards

TABLE OF CONTENTS

Table of Contents

Table of Contents

Table of Contents

PREFACE

"The things I want to know are in books," Abraham Lincoln wrote, and so he read.

Lincoln not only taught himself to read, but he also took reading and the books he read seriously. In his late thirties, for instance, when Lincoln wanted to sharpen his powers of reasoning after having served a term in Congress, he read—and mastered—the first six books of Euclid. "My best friend," he went on, "is the man who'll get me a book I ain't read."

Likewise, consider George Washington, perhaps the least educated of the Founders. He, too, maintained a lifelong course of self-education. As events developed, he focused on learning the major political writings of the day—those of Tom Paine, John Adams, Thomas Jefferson, James Madison, and the various Revolutionary authors—not to mention contemporary books like Adam Smith's *Wealth of Nations* and even classic works such as those of the Roman orator Cicero. "A knowledge of books," he observed, "is the basis on which all other knowledge rests."

My favorite example of the book-and-greatness genre is that of a lieutenant in the 4th Hussars of the British military. It was in 1896, thousands of miles away from home in India, that 22-year-old Winston Churchill (who had been a less than stellar student in school) decided he was "wanting in even the vaguest knowledge about many large spheres of thought" and "resolved to read history, philosophy, economics, and things like that" in order to prepare himself for public life. And so he followed a regimen over the next several years, sometimes reading four or five hours a day, to familiarize himself with standard works, from *The Politics* of Aristotle to Gibbon's *Decline and Fall of the Roman Empire*. "It was a curious education," he recollected. "I approached it with an empty, hungry mind, and with fairly strong jaws; and what I got I bit."

There will always be something about a good old print-on-paper book, even in this time of computers, the Internet, iPods, and blogs, that brings the reader into conversation with the author better than any other medium. That's why the greatest books will undoubtedly remain the key to an education that is liberating of the mind and enriching of the soul.

But there is also an important connection, not to be overlooked, between books and democracy. This is because popular government requires an engaged and educated citizenry that knows and understands the rights and responsibilities of self-government and statesmen who not only are good citizens, but also possess the prudential wisdom to govern—knowing when to act and for what purpose. And that kind of knowledge, and much of that wisdom, is to be found primarily in books, portraying citizens and statesmen, thinkers and doers, in biography, history, literature, and the like.

What follows is a practical list of thoughtful books (not "the classics"—which supposedly are covered in a standard liberal arts education—but solidly good books) recommended to guide intelligent, conservative-minded readers who want to prepare themselves for a public life of thought and action and so seek to know more about history, politics, literature, economics, statesmanship, religion, public policy, and modern conservative thought. Edited and annotated by Lee Edwards, our own Distinguished Fellow in Conservative Thought, the list is not intended to be definitive, or comprehensive, or followed in any particular order, but rather to provide a general framework around which the reader can build a firmer structure of political knowledge.

This publication is part of a series of essays and occasional booklets published by The Heritage Foundation, under the auspices of the B. Kenneth Simon Center for American Studies, on the "First Principles" of the American tradition of liberty that we seek to conserve "for ourselves and our posterity," as it says in our Constitution. The publications cover a range of themes and topics, each aimed at explaining core ideas—which often have been forgotten or rejected—and considering what they mean for America today.

The core idea here is that books contain the ideas, make the arguments, and preserve the history necessary for the maintenance and perpetuation of freedom.

"I cannot live without books," proclaimed Thomas Jefferson. To a previous generation, this was, shall we say, self-evident. Books were a mirror of the past and a window to the future. "I have read my eyes out and can't read half enough," John Adams once lamented in a letter to Abigail. "*The more one reads, the more one sees we have to read.*"

Good books are rightly addictive, enticing the dedicated reader to open more books and gain more knowledge and come closer to wisdom. And so I invite you to read on, and on.

Matthew Spalding
Director, B. Kenneth Simon Center for American Studies
First Principles Series Editor

INTRODUCTION

*R*eading the Right Books rests on the premise that books can change a life and even the course of history. I can personally attest that they made a profound difference in the life of Ronald Reagan.

In mid-October of 1965, my wife Anne and I spent two days traveling with Reagan in Southern California when he was considering whether to run for governor. We were with Reagan early and late—at a Rotary breakfast, a Kiwanis lunch, a Republican women's brunch, an evening address to a businessmen's convention. He never seemed to tire, perspire, or stop smiling. There was about him the unmistakable aura of a star and a leader.

At the end of the first day, back in our motel, Anne (who had acquired considerable political experience as a Young Republican leader in New York City) looked at me, and I looked at her, and we both said at the same time, "He's got it!"

At the end of the second day, Reagan took us up the steep winding road to his home in Pacific Palisades overlooking Los Angeles for iced tea and cookies. While he and Nancy were in the kitchen, I walked over to the bookcases in their library-den and began examining the titles. They were, almost without exception, works of history, economics, and politics. They included conservative classics such as F. A. Hayek's *The Road to*

Serfdom, Whittaker Chambers' *Witness*, Henry Hazlitt's *Economics in One Lesson*, and Frederic Bastiat's *The Law*.

I opened several books. They were dog-eared and annotated, obviously read more than once. Here was the personal library of a serious, thoughtful individual who had arrived at his conservatism the old-fashioned way: through study and reflection, one book at a time. That night I wrote in my notebook: "President Reagan?"

Reading the Right Books: A Heritage Guide for the Intelligent Conservative is an annotated list of 101 books published after 1900 that a conservative can profitably read to further the right ideas in his life and work. (There is only one exception to our post-1900 rule: Frederick Douglass's amazing autobiography, first published in 1845.) The *Guide* is intended primarily for congressional staffers, young professionals, and undergraduate students, but it can be consulted by conservatives of all ages and, indeed, all Americans who believe in ordered liberty.

While there are several excellent conservative book lists, such as the "50 Best" and the "50 Worst" books of the 20th century suggested by the Intercollegiate Studies Institute and the "100 Best Non-Fiction Books" of the century published by *National Review*, *Reading the Right Books* is more than a list. It explains the relevance of each recommended book to American conservatism and gives a brief summary of its contents.

Another difference is that the list in *Reading the Right Books* is divided into 12 categories so that you, the reader, may choose to read books in those areas in which you are most interested or in which you would like to improve your understanding. The categories are World History, American History, Conservative Thought, Economics, World Politics, Totalitarianism, Religion, Political Culture, Public Policy, Statesmanship, Unconventional Thought, and Literature.

Reading the Right Books places an emphasis on books concerned with politics—thus, the categories of American History, Conservative Thought, Economics, and Statesmanship (including biographies of great conservatives like Ronald Reagan and Winston Churchill). But you will note the categories of Unconventional Thought and Literature. The former includes a candid memoir by David Horowitz, who reveals why he went from Left to Right, and a scathing satire of the federal government by P. J. O'Rourke (demonstrating yet again that conservatives have a well-developed sense of humor). We included a Literature category because the impact of fiction, of a novel like *1984* by George Orwell or *Atlas Shrugged* by Ayn Rand, can be significant and lasting.

The *Heritage Guide* is not a list of the great books of Western civilization. We assume that, in the course of your liberal education, you have read at least portions of such classics as Homer's *Iliad* and Thucydides' *History of the Peloponnesian War* as well as Plato's *The Republic*, Saint Augustine's *The Confessions*, Machiavelli's *The Prince*, and Adam Smith's *The Wealth of Nations*.

We also assume that you are familiar with the classics of the American tradition, such as the Declaration of Independence, the Constitution, *The Federalist*, George Washington's Farewell Address, and Alexis de Tocqueville's *Democracy in America*.

Not all of the books in our *Guide* are conservative books or written by conservatives, but every book will deepen your appreciation of conservatism. *Reading the Right Books* aims to help fill the gaps in history, politics, economics, and similar areas created by the politically correct, illiberal education of too many colleges and universities.

We firmly believe in the ability of books to inspire and motivate. Without Karl Marx's *The Communist Manifesto*, for example, Marxism might have remained an obscure theory and not produced the deaths of an estimated 100 million victims in the 20th century.

Without Thomas Paine's *Common Sense*, the American colonists might not have been inspired to challenge the greatest military power on Earth and win their independence.

Without Russell Kirk's *The Conservative Mind*, conservatism might have remained unaware of its intellectual heritage, and the conservative movement might have remained nameless.

Some post-Gutenberg modernists argue that new media such as the Internet have rendered books irrelevant. You often hear the dismissive comment, "No one has time to read a book anymore." We disagree. A recent Heritage survey as well as our own poll of conservative leaders revealed that books made a powerful difference in their thinking, continuing to resonate throughout their lives.

Henry Hazlitt's *Economics in One Lesson*, said Sally Pipes of the Pacific Research Institute, was not part of her college curriculum, but "it gave credence to my own views which on campus were seen as unpopular and even radical. It served as a guiding light not only throughout college but throughout my career."

"Every American student should read *One Day in the Life of Ivan Denisovich* by Alexander Solzhenitsyn," said Paul Gigot of *The Wall Street Journal*, "to understand why we fought the Cold War. And why we won it."

Barry Goldwater's *The Conscience of a Conservative*, responded John Goodman of the National Center for Public Policy, "laid the foundation for all that's good and worthwhile in the modern conservative movement."

We do not share the apparent enthusiasm of *The New York Times* for "a universal library" on the Internet, as described by Kevin Kelly of *Wired* magazine. The universal library, exults Kelly, will encourage the creation of virtual "bookshelves"—a collection of texts, some as short as a paragraph, others as long as entire books. Once created, these "bookshelves" will be published and swapped in the public commons. "Indeed," writes Kelly, "some authors will begin to write books to be read as snippets or to be remixed as pages."

Among those who shared our horror at such intellectual mutilation was novelist John Updike, who argued that "the printed, bound and paid-for book was—still is, for the moment—more exacting, more demanding of its producer and consumer both." We cannot allow the intellectual revolution which has, since the Renaissance, taught men and women to cherish and cultivate their individuality, Updike said, to "end in a sparkling cloud of snippets."

Reading the Right Books is our response to the idea of a universal library of snippets.

Our list of 101 books is the end product of a months-long process of deliberation and decision-making. We sent questionnaires to 50 prominent conservatives, asking them to give us one or two titles in each category and to explain why they suggested them. We reduced the resulting list of over 300 titles to 150 and held an all-day meeting of editorial advisers with the goal of arriving at a final list of 100 books. We wound up with 108 titles that were reduced by seven in the writing and editing of the annotations.

The distinguished members of our editorial advisory board are Charles Kesler, editor of the *Claremont Review of Books*; Michael Potemra, literary editor of *National Review*; Joseph Bottum, editor of *First Things*; Alfred Regnery, publisher of *The American Spectator*; John O'Sullivan, editor-at-large of *National Review*; Philip Terzian, books and arts editor of *The Weekly Standard*; Matthew Spalding, director of the Center for American Studies at The Heritage Foundation; and Lee Edwards, Distinguished Fellow in Conservative Thought at

The Heritage Foundation. Exceedingly helpful in the research and editing of the annotations were Heritage interns T. Kenneth Cribb II, Alan Orrison, Catherine Mancusi, Sandra Czelusniak, and Bronson Kopp as well as the omnicompetent Carolyn Garris, program coordinator of the Center for American Studies at Heritage.

In deciding whether or not a book furthered conservative ideas, we were guided by the basic principles set forth in the mission of The Heritage Foundation: free enterprise, limited government, individual freedom, traditional American values, and a strong national defense.

We hope you find our *Guide* useful. It is not meant to be definitive. We hope our suggestions will prompt you to go out and read far beyond our list of 101 books.

We have included tried and true classics such as Whittaker Chambers' autobiography *Witness* and Richard Weaver's *Ideas Have Consequences*. We have also suggested books not usually found on a conservative book list such as *A Man of the People*, Alonzo Hamby's illuminating biography of Harry Truman, and Ralph Ellison's haunting novel, *Invisible Man*.

Because this is a *Heritage Guide for the Intelligent Conservative*, we do not propose a list of books to be read and stop there. Here are some suggestions on *how* to read the books in our *Guide*.

To begin with, choose the books carefully and according to your needs. Do not try to read all 101 titles in *Reading the Right Books* in one month or even one year. Take advantage of, and spend time with, the writers who most appeal to you.

Do not accept unthinkingly everything that an author writes. A book is a stimulant to our thinking, the classical scholar A. D. Sortillanges says; "it is not a substitute and it is not a chain."

A successful reading plan requires three things, according to Georgetown University professor James V. Schall: a sense of self-discipline, a personal library, and good guides. We would add that you also need a good lamp, a comfortable chair, and your favorite non-alcoholic beverage.

Self-discipline is not a popular virtue in these modern times, even for conservatives; but self-discipline—the ability to apply oneself to a goal—is vital if we want to learn what is really important and to apply that knowledge in our lives.

All kinds of things will get in the way of self-discipline, Schall warns: things like "drink or drugs or television or parties or work or our own laziness or an *eros* untempered by any sense of justice, friendship, duty, purpose, or permanence." But these things can be controlled and overcome through a greater desire—the desire to learn and to understand ourselves and our world.

The second requirement for a reading plan is a personal library. Modern computers give us millions of bytes of information in a short accessible form. We are fortunate, says Schall, to have almost all of the world's books, music, art, journals, and press available to us through the Internet. Nevertheless, "the most important ideas and concepts still appear first in the print media, in books."

But it is not necessary, or possible, either to read *every* good book or to have a large personal library. Schall suggests that you collect a few books, perhaps a dozen or two, and get to know them well. C. S. Lewis observed that we have not read a great book at all if we have read it only once.

The building of even a small personal library will take time and thought. It will be impeded by the fact, as Schall puts it, that we live in an age that is reluctant to accept, if not hostile to, the idea that some things—such as books—are better than others, "some things closer to the spirit of *what is*." But conservatives know, as Russell Kirk wrote, that "sound books about the human condition and about the civil social order" can arouse "a healthy intellectual reaction to preserve order, justice, and freedom."

Once you have selected the books and they are on your shelves, they will be like your best friends: trustworthy and unchanging, able to help you think through the most important questions.

The third requirement for a reading plan is good guides. They may be your teachers, your colleagues, your friends, or your family members. They may be book lists like *Reading the Right Books*. You may encounter a guide in unexpected places. A good book about the dangers of ideology is *The True Believer* by Eric Hoffer, a self-educated longshoreman.

One of the best books about reading is Mortimer Adler's *How to Read a Book*, first published in 1940 and revised and updated several times since. It is filled with useful maxims such as:

- Passive reading is impossible: "We cannot read with our eyes immobilized and our minds asleep."
- Every book should be read no more slowly than it deserves and no more quickly than you can read it with satisfaction and comprehension.
- Do not try to understand every word or page of a difficult book the first time through.
- Writing your reactions down (in the book or separately) helps you remember the thoughts of the author. (Ronald Reagan certainly followed this advice.)
- Books, especially of history and philosophy, should be read in relation to each other. For example, you cannot understand *The Federalist Papers* without having first read the Declaration of Independence and the U.S. Constitution. You can better appreciate Catherine Drinker Bowen's *Mira-*

cle at Philadelphia if you have first read *The Birth of the Republic* by Edmund Morgan.

- The best books reward you in two ways: there is the improvement in your reading skill that occurs when you tackle a difficult work; and, more important, you become wiser about yourself and "the great and enduring truths of human life."

We know that *Reading the Right Books* will stimulate various responses. Some of you will plunge right in and begin reading, perhaps two or three books at the same time. Others will ponder before selecting one book and limiting themselves to reading a few pages each day. Both ways of reading are good if they enable the individual reader to become, as Richard Weaver put it, "something better than he would have been without it."

What difference can books make? We like the answer suggested by Jeffrey O. Nelson, the president of Thomas More College: "Books of the right kind by men and women of imagination and perception are indispensable for the flourishing of order, freedom, justice, and the authentic progress of civilization."

So, let the reading begin.

Lee Edwards
Editor

CONSERVATIVE THOUGHT

*M*ore so than any other political movement in American history, the modern conservative movement is guided not by political goals but by ideas, confident that the right ideas will lead over time to the right political outcomes. Among conservatism's core principles are a firm belief in limited constitutional government; a conviction that freedom produces prosperity, opportunity, and a civil society; and a belief in a transcendent moral order.

This category encompasses the core writers of post–World War II conservative thought—from traditionalist Russell Kirk to classical liberal F. A Hayek and neoconservative Irving Kristol—reflecting the diversity within conservatism and its commitment to the preservation of ordered liberty.

The Road to Serfdom, F. A. Hayek (1944)

In the spring of 1945, the whole world seemed to be turning Left. Eastern Europe had been ceded to Communism, Western Europe was dominated by socialist ideas, Mao Zedong was preparing to launch a civil war that would bring China into the Communist camp, and President Harry Truman was expected to carry forward the late Franklin D. Roosevelt's welfarist New Deal policies. In that hour of overweening statism, the Austrian economist F. A. Hayek published a little book, *The Road to Serfdom*, which laid the foundation for an intellectual and political counterrevolution.

Hayek argues that planning leads to dictatorship and that the direction of economic activity inevitably means the suppression of freedom. In *The Road to Serfdom*, he describes the disturbing signs of collectivism all around him and proposes a different road—the road of individualism and classical liberalism. Hayek describes the personal virtues necessary to travel that road: independence and self-reliance, individual initiative and local responsibility, and "a healthy suspicion of power and authority." He emphasizes that he is not advocating a dogmatic *laissez-faire* attitude. Like the classical political economist Adam Smith, Hayek accepts a governmental role, carefully limited by law, that encourages competition and the functioning of a free society.

Described by *The New York Times* as "one of the most important books of our generation," the work attained bestseller status through a condensed edition in *Reader's Digest* and the distribution of a million copies of the *Digest* version by the Book of the Month Club. Hayek's "little book" was the first defining philosophical work of the modern American conservative movement.

Ideas Have Consequences, Richard M. Weaver (1948)

For many, *Ideas Have Consequences* is the *fons et origo* (source and origin) of the American conservative movement. Here, Richard M. Weaver traces the dissolution of Western thought and culture to the 14th century when the West abandoned its belief in transcendental values and accepted man as "the measure of all things." Religious practice declined, and a faith in scientific rationalism ultimately triumphed. Weaver argues that by 1948, when *Ideas Have Consequences* was published, civilization faced rampant egalitarianism and the cult of the masses, the result of centuries of retreat from first principles and true knowledge.

Yet, as historian George Nash points out, it was not Weaver's intention to write a jeremiad. The University of Chicago literature professor offers three proposals for reform. First, we must defend the right of private property—"the last metaphysical right remaining to us." Second, our language must be purified and rescued from "the impulse to dissolve everything into sensation." Third, we must adopt an attitude of "piety" toward nature, other human beings, and the past. Such piety, Weaver says, will serve as at least a partial antidote for modern man's egotism, "hysterical optimism," and "war against substance."

The parallels between the traditional conservative Weaver and the classical liberal F. A. Hayek are instructive. Both Weaver and Hayek attribute the decline of the West to "pernicious" liberal ideas. For Hayek, it is economic planning; for Weaver, it is moral relativism. Hayek proposes the alternative road of individual freedom within a framework of carefully limited government. Weaver insists that a good society requires a foundation of certain eternal truths. Both men provide a conservative answer to the twin threats of statism at home and socialism abroad.

Memoirs of a Superfluous Man, Albert Jay Nock (1943)

Conservatives have always admired the fiercely independent intellectual who sticks by his ideas regardless of whether they are out of step with the times. Author-editor Albert Jay Nock was a radical libertarian of the 1920s and 1930s whose denunciations of the State and of unbridled materialism influenced such leading figures of the post-war Right as Russell Kirk, William F. Buckley Jr., Robert Nisbet, and Frank Chodorov. They were drawn by his mocking wit—he once wrote that dogs were "natural-born New Dealers"—and responded to his call to preach the gospel of individual freedom, trusting that a "remnant" would one day build a new and free society.

In *Memoirs of a Superfluous Man*, Nock reveals himself to be passionate in his anti-statism, unyielding in his love for the classics and traditional education, and scornful of the uneducable masses. He invents what he calls "Epstein's Law" as an explanation of human activity: "Man tends always to satisfy his needs with the least possible exertion." He holds out little hope for any effective political reform. At the same time, however, Nock's memoir resonates with the conviction that, like the prophet Isaiah of the 8th century BC, modern-day Isaiahs have the duty to proclaim the truth about man, the state, and liberty.

God and Man at Yale: The Superstitions of "Academic Freedom," William F. Buckley Jr. (1951)

The struggle for the minds and souls of our colleges and universities has been waged for decades. More than half a century ago, a recent college graduate offered a searing critique of his alma mater, charging that its values were agnostic as to religion, "interventionist" and Keynesian as to economics, and collectivist as regards the relation of the individual to society and government. While conceding the validity of academic freedom for a professor's research, he insisted that the professor did not have the right to inseminate values into the minds of his students that were counter to the values of the parents paying his salary. He urged parents, alumni, and trustees to resist this aberrant form of academic freedom. The university administration and its supporters erupted, heaping bitter invective upon the author, calling his book "dishonest," "ignorant," and reminiscent of "a fiery cross on a hillside."

The alumnus was William F. Buckley Jr., the university was Yale, and American politics has not been the same since. At 26, the future founding editor of *National Review* and author of dozens of best-selling books was already outrageous and courageous. Here, Buckley charges that Yale has abandoned both Christianity and free enterprise or what he calls "individualism." He says that the faculty members who foster atheism and socialism ought to be fired. He argues that the primary goal of education is to familiarize students with an existing body of truth, of which Christianity and free enterprise are the foundations. But, Buckley reports, "individualism is dying at Yale, and without a fight."

That is no longer true in the American academy. Conservatives picked up the gauntlet thrown down by Buckley and began to defend individualism on a thousand campuses. The battle for true academic freedom, launched by Buckley's best-selling book, continues to this day.

The Conservative Mind: From Burke to Santayana, Russell Kirk (1953)

When *The Conservative Mind* was published in 1953, liberal intellectuals smirked that the title was an oxymoron, but they stopped laughing when they read Russell Kirk's brilliant overview of Anglo–American conservative thinking over the past 175 years. They were also stunned by a defiant indictment of every liberal nostrum from human perfectibility to economic egalitarianism.

The conservatives that Kirk presents with such enthusiasm include the British politician Edmund Burke, the founder of "the true school of conservative thinking," as well as Sir Walter

Scott, Samuel Taylor Coleridge, Benjamin Disraeli, and John Henry Newman in Britain and the Adams family (especially John), Nathaniel Hawthorne, Orestes Brownson, Irving Babbitt, and Paul Elmer More in America.

While other conservatives may protest that no definition is possible, Kirk declares that the essence of conservatism lies in six canons: (1) a divine intent, as well as personal conscience, rules society; (2) traditional life is filled with variety and mystery, while most radical systems are characterized by a narrowing conformity; (3) civilized society requires order and hierarchy; (4) property and freedom are inseparably connected; (5) man must control his will and his appetite, knowing that he is governed more by emotion than reason; and (6) society must alter slowly.

Never out of print since its publication over half a century ago, *The Conservative Mind* made conservatism intellectually respectable and gave the conservative movement its name.

In Defense of Freedom: A Conservative Credo, Frank S. Meyer (1962)

One conservative more than any other in the early years of the modern conservative movement attempted to reconcile the philosophical differences between traditional conservatives and libertarians: Frank Meyer, a senior editor of *National Review*. Meyer was an individualist who argued that "freedom of the person" was the primary end of political action. The State has only three strictly limited functions: national defense, the preservation of domestic order, and the administration of justice between individuals. The "achievement of virtue," he insisted, is not the State's business; individuals should be left alone to work out their own salvation. But Meyer was a political activist as well as a political philosopher who understood that the conservative movement needed both traditionalists and libertarians to become politically successful.

In his most important book, *In Defense of Freedom*, Meyer writes that "the Christian understanding of the nature and destiny of man" is what conservatives are trying to preserve. Both traditionalists and libertarians should therefore acknowledge the true heritage of the West: "reason operating within tradition." This approach was dubbed "fusionism," which Meyer said was based on the conservative consensus already forged by the Founders at the Constitutional Convention of 1787.

Meyer's nuanced fusionism of freedom and order was sharply criticized by conservative intellectuals of all shades. Russell Kirk accused Meyer of "detesting" all champions of authority. A prominent student of F. A. Hayek complained that Meyer failed to state *what* tradition conservatives should follow. But as historian George Nash points out, fusionism became the *de facto* consensus of the conservative movement. Frank Meyer, wrote one scholar, was "the first conservative theorist" to comprehend the uniqueness of American conservatism and to explain its uniqueness to the conservative rank and file.

The Conscience of a Conservative, Barry Goldwater (1960)

Senator Barry Goldwater of Arizona, the 1964 Republican candidate for President, was, in the words of columnist George Will, "a man who lost forty-four states but won the future." His historic campaign actually began four years earlier with the publication of a little book that takes only an hour to read but whose liberating ideas remain with the reader. *The Conscience of a Conservative* sold more than 3.5 million copies, making it one of the most widely read political manifestos of modern times.

In the first pages, Goldwater dismisses the idea that conservatism is out of date, arguing that such a statement is like saying that "the Golden Rule or the Ten Commandments or Aristotle's *Politics* are out of date." The conservative approach, he explains, "is nothing more or less than an attempt to apply the wisdom of experience and the revealed truths of the past to the problems of today." Unlike the liberal, the conservative believes that man is not only an economic, but also a spiritual creature. Indeed, Goldwater says, the first obligation of a political thinker is "to understand the nature of man."

In *The Conscience of a Conservative*, Goldwater addresses the issues that have dominated the national debate for decades. Taxes? Flatten them. Government spending? Eliminate programs better handled by the states, private institutions, or individuals. Social Security? Strengthen it by introducing a voluntary option. Law and order? The rights of victims should always take precedence over those of criminals. Communism? Why not victory?

Deeply concerned about the tendency to concentrate power in the hands of a few, Goldwater was convinced that most Americans wanted to reverse the trend. The transition will come, he writes, when the people entrust their affairs to those "who understand that their first duty as public officials is to divest themselves of the power they have been given." The people must elect candidates who boldly proclaim, "My aim is not to pass laws, but to repeal them." *The Conscience of a Conservative* is an essential work by a founding father of the modern conservative movement.

The Quest for Community: A Study in the Ethics of Order and Freedom, Robert Nisbet (1953)

Man's fundamental desire for community, argues sociologist Robert Nisbet in this conservative classic, cannot be satisfied either by the centralized state or by unrestrained individualism. He quotes Thomas Jefferson's shrewd observation that a state with the power to do things *for* people has the power to do things *to* them. Many individualists, Nisbet argues, fail to recognize the close dependence of their thought on "the subtle, infinitely complex lines of habit, tradition, and social relationship." What is needed is a middle way that, as a practical matter, contents itself with "the setting of human life, not human life itself."

Nisbet, who spent most of his life teaching in the California university system, maintains that the quest for community cannot be denied, for it springs from some of the most powerful needs of human nature, including "a clear sense of cultural purpose, membership, status, and continuity." It should be the prime business of any serious conservative group, he says, to work tirelessly toward the diminution of the unitary state and to nurture the varied groups and intermediating associations that form "the true building blocks of the social order."

When *The Quest for Community* appeared in 1953, American liberals dismissed it because they were wed to the idea of "a national community," while many libertarians paid it scant attention because they favored a radical individualism as protection against the totalitarian state. But Russell Kirk and other traditional conservatives warmly praised its core message: In order to live in freedom, man must break the bonds between himself and the state through a revitalization of intermediate associations such as the family, the church, and the neighborhood—the "little platoons of life" about which Edmund Burke wrote so eloquently. Nisbet's work, reviving and deepening a Tocquevillian understanding of the role played by non-governmental institutions, also helped to inspire the civil society movement within conservatism.

Reagan, In His Own Hand: The Writings of Ronald Reagan That Reveal His Revolutionary Vision for America, ed. Kiron K. Skinner, Annelise Anderson, Martin Anderson (2001)

Some presidential myths die hard. One of the more persistent about Ronald Reagan is that he was essentially an amiable dunce heavily dependent on advisers and speechwriters for his thoughts and words. On the contrary, Reagan possessed an inquisitive, far-ranging mind and was deeply interested all his life in history, economics, and politics. Furthermore, he had the ability to take complex issues and ideas and to discuss them in clear, concise language. Indisputable proof of Reagan's high intelligence and exceptional writing skill can be found in this work, a selection of 670 radio commentaries the future President personally wrote and delivered between 1975 and 1979.

The commentaries reveal Reagan's conservative vision for America: a vision of faith and freedom that would restore Americans' confidence in themselves and their country, produce the longest peacetime economic expansion in U.S. history, and end the Cold War in victory for the West. The main goal of America's foreign policy, Reagan argued, should be not to contain, but to defeat Communism through a strong military and support of the "captive nations" behind the Iron Curtain. In the area of domestic policy, Reagan stressed the importance of tax cuts and less government regulation. He called for judges who respected rather than reinterpreted the Constitution. He criticized, for example, the Supreme Court's decision to "expel" God from the public schools, commenting,

"One wonders how a teacher would answer if a student asked why it was called Christmas."

The late 1970s were a time of pessimism for many Americans, engendered by low economic growth, high unemployment and inflation, and Communism's aggressive thrust into Latin America, Africa, and Asia. But Reagan had no doubts about the future: "I am more convinced than ever," he declared, "of the greatness of our people and their capacity to determine their own destiny." *Reagan, In His Own Hand* provides a revealing profile of a remarkable conservative mind.

Neoconservatism: The Autobiography of an Idea, Irving Kristol (1995)

No one disputes that "neoconservatism" is an integral part of the American conservative movement; some would even call it indispensable. But just what is neoconservatism? Who is behind it, and how has it come to play such a critical role in American politics?

In *Neoconservatism: The Autobiography of an Idea,* Irving Kristol traces how a series of events in the late 1960s and early 1970s jolted a small but influential group of old-fashioned liberals and forced them to move out of their no-longer-comfortable Democratic digs. The cataclysmic happenings included the presidential candidacy of leftist George McGovern, the willingness of modern liberals to let Vietnam and other nations under siege fall into the hands of the Communists, the refusal of prominent Democrats to condemn the U.N. for its virulent anti-Israel rhetoric, and the revolution in social and sexual relations that produced the "adversary culture."

"Mugged by reality" (Kristol's phrase), the neoconservatives attacked the radicals as despoilers of the liberal tradition. Led by their grand strategist Kristol, the neoconservatives called for a return to the "republican virtue" of the Founding

Fathers and invoked the ideal of a good society. The former leftists conceded that a "hidden hand" has its uses in the marketplace, culminating in Kristol's utterance, "two cheers for capitalism." The neoconservatives were "action intellectuals" with connections to America's leading universities and the mass media, direct access to the political elite, and strong roots in influential foundations and think tanks. They carried the conservative message to places where no traditional conservative had gone before.

Kristol writes with ease, clarity, and humor in these essays that show his gradual development from youthful Trotskyite to staunch Cold War liberal to benevolent godfather of neoconservatism, which, he says, has been absorbed into a "larger more comprehensive conservatism." He leaves ultimate evaluation to historians but insists that the "neoconservative enterprise" was needed to "enliven American conservatism and help reshape American politics."

The Conservative Intellectual Movement in America Since 1945, George H. Nash (1976)

Indispensable to an understanding of modern American conservatism is George H. Nash's *The Conservative Intellectual Movement in America Since 1945*. Part history, part biography, and part philosophical primer, Nash's book shows how a brilliant and diverse group of scholars and writers—traditional conservatives, libertarians, and anti-Communists—slowly came together and by the 1960s had formed an intellectual movement. The glue that held these disparate intellectuals together was the external threat of Soviet Communism along with a deep antipathy toward 20th century liberalism. They were joined by leaders of neoconservatism and the Religious Right, producing a powerful intellectual force in America. With the Reagan Revolution of the 1980s, the nation witnessed the phenomenon, Nash writes, of "the passage of an idea from theory to practice" at the highest level of government.

In a very real sense, *The Conservative Intellectual Movement in America Since 1945* is an encyclopedia. Nash provides a *précis* of the most important works of the most influential conservative thinkers and writers of the past 50 years, including Russell Kirk, F. A. Hayek, Richard Weaver, Whittaker Chambers, Milton Friedman, Ludwig von Mises, Irving Kristol, Leo Strauss, Eric Voegelin, James Burnham, and William F. Buckley, along with personal insights into the authors.

The Italian writer Mazzini once said, "Ideas rule the world and its events." Nash's magisterial work is a must-read for the intelligent conservative who wants to understand why the idea of conservatism now dominates much of America's politics.

ECONOMICS

$\int$ ince the founding of the Republic, there has been a sharp political debate over the role of the federal government in the economy. Among the issues in 1790 were a call for a national bank and the question of whether to raise tariffs. In the 20th century, following the Great Depression, liberals urged and conservatives resisted the creation of a welfare state. In the past quarter of a century, conservatives have led a counteroffensive against federal regulations and expenditures, but the ever-increasing size of government leaves the outcome in doubt.

In the category of ECONOMICS, we offer works by 10 of the leading (and most comprehensible) free-market economists in the world, including Nobel Prize winner Milton Friedman, Bradley Prize winners Thomas Sowell and Hernando de Soto, and Templeton Prize winner Michael Novak. If you read all of the books, you will have a good understanding of what Adam Smith called the "invisible hand"—how each individual promotes the general welfare when he seeks to advance his own welfare.

***Economics in One Lesson: The Shortest and Surest Way to Understand Basic Economics*, Henry Hazlitt (1946)**

There are only a few volumes that can be considered great introductions to economics: Frederic Bastiat's *Economic Harmo-*

nies, the first dozen chapters of Adam Smith's *Wealth of Nations*, and Philip Wicksteed's *The Alphabet of Economic Science* all come to mind. No short list would be complete without *Economics in One Lesson* by the long-time economics correspondent for *Newsweek* and *The New York Times*, Henry Hazlitt. It is not too much to claim that this little book may be the most influential overview of economics published since World War II.

The book's theme is as relevant today as when it was first published: Government's economic actions frequently have long-term consequences that are the opposite of what policy-makers intended. As Bastiat would put it, there is that which is seen and that which is unseen, and the latter is ultimately more important. Through a series of eye-catching illustrations, Hazlitt shows that the effect of well-intentioned policies often is to harm the economy and the people that government started out to help.

Public-sector spending intended to stimulate a sluggish economy may result in higher taxes to pay for that spending, which actually slows the economy. Public works programs take valuable resources out of private hands, reducing the ability of the private sector to create wealth in the long run. Governments impose rent controls to protect certain citizens, but a price ceiling discourages landlords from maintaining their properties at a proper level. The quantity as well as the quality of available housing falls, hurting the "protected" citizens worse than if their rents had been increased.

The lessons of *Economics in One Lesson* have improved public policy over the past 60 years. Even so, the sorry state of most economic policies shows how much improvement is needed over the next 60 years. Hazlitt's commonsense book remains useful to those who are seeking to reform our badly misdirected economic institutions and practices.

Liberalism: A Socio-Economic Exposition,
Ludwig von Mises (1978 edition)

One of the greatest "liberals" of the 20th century was one of the greatest opponents of big government and the welfare state. Ludwig von Mises spent his enormously productive life expanding our knowledge of social and economic orders founded on individual liberty, pitting him against the most determined proponents of state power in human history.

Liberalism, first published in German in the 1920s, is a comprehensive exposition of the whole tree of liberty, from the philosophical roots of the free society (property rights, equality before the law, individual liberty, and so forth) to the branches of public policy that give our world its social and economic shape (foreign policy, taxation, free trade, economic regulation, and many other topics).

Readers of this remarkable book of only 200 pages will learn, for example, that a true liberal foreign policy encourages peaceful, productive relationships among countries. Mises shows that a foreign policy built on free trade, self-determination, and respect for private property discourages war and promotes the economic and social institutions that make war less likely.

Equally powerful is the case Mises makes for a domestic "liberal" order. Again, the expansion and defense of private property encourages the growth of economic and social liberty and constrains the exercise of government's police powers. Classical liberalism's great contribution to human well-being, Mises shows, has been the limits it has placed on state action.

Liberalism is one of the definitive works in political and economic theory. Students of every discipline, not just politics and economics, would be well served by savoring the liberal wisdom of Ludwig von Mises, who, among other things, was the teacher and mentor of Nobel laureate F. A. Hayek.

Capitalism and Freedom, Milton Friedman (1962)

Milton Friedman, long-time professor of economics at the University of Chicago, launches his ardent defense of liberty in *Capitalism and Freedom* with a criticism of President John Kennedy's neo-Keynesian call to "ask what you can do for your country." Instead, Friedman proposes that "we take freedom of the individual, or perhaps of the family, as our ultimate goal in judging social arrangements." His reasons are practical and compelling: Social progress results from a climate of variety and diversity, and free markets are a necessary condition for political freedom. "Democratic socialism" can never be truly democratic. Most important, freedom and justice must work together, rewarding merit and allowing for coordination without coercion.

Friedman is careful to note that while freedom is the highest goal of society, it cannot be the highest goal of individuals. Freedom in and of itself is not "an all-embracing ethic," he writes. "The really important ethical problems are those that face an individual in a free society—what he should do with his freedom." Economic and social freedom, Friedman argues, is not a state of nature or a state of grace. Rather, freedom creates the space within which individuals can make their own choices.

As a groundbreaking scholar, influential teacher, best-selling author, and adviser to Presidents and prime ministers, Milton Friedman defended the efficiency of the free market and the justice to be found in freedom. *Capitalism and Freedom* is the *summa* of the man who, in the words of *The Economist*, was "the greatest economist of the 20th century."

FDR's Folly: How Roosevelt and His New Deal Prolonged the Great Depression, Jim Powell (2003)

Although liberal historians like Arthur Schlesinger, Jr., and James MacGregor Burns have credited President Franklin D. Roosevelt's New Deal with being the primary means by which America emerged from the Great Depression of the 1930s, there is now a large body of convincing evidence that the New Deal prolonged rather than shortened the nation's most serious economic crisis.

Consider these facts: From 1934 to 1940, the median annual unemployment rate was 17.2 percent. The recovery peak in 1937 was followed by another debilitating crash. FDR tripled federal taxes, reducing the amount of money in people's pockets as well as the capital needed for businesses to create jobs. New Deal agricultural policies helped big farmers with the most acreage and output rather than small family farmers. FDR doubled federal spending, but unemployment remained stubbornly high. It is critical to know the facts about the New Deal lest, in a future recession or depression, policymakers repeat the mistakes of FDR's seriously flawed economic plan.

Drawing on the major findings of economists over the past several decades, *FDR's Folly* shows how the New Deal promoted cartels, imposed confiscatory taxes, made it harder for companies to raise capital, made it more expensive for businesses to employ people, and bombarded industries with dubious antitrust lawsuits. Powell quotes the Pulitzer Prize–winning historian David M. Kennedy, who wrote that whatever it was, the New Deal "was not a recovery program." Crisply written and solidly researched, *FDR's Folly* affirms that a government can best promote a speedy economic recovery by letting people keep more of their money, removing obstacles to "productive enterprise," and providing "a political climate where investors feel that it's safe to invest for the future."

A Humane Economy: The Social Framework of the Free Market, Wilhelm Roepke (1960)

After World War II, when many European intellectuals were singing the praises of statism, the German economist Wilhelm Roepke denounced the fundamental immorality of all planned economies and challenged those who insisted that socialist regimes were the wave of the future. His views were vindicated when the West German minister of economics, Ludwig Erhard, adopted a free-market economy at Roepke's urging, launching a remarkable post-war recovery. Roepke's critics hailed the recovery as a "miracle" when it was the logical outcome of free-market policies. Encouraged by the results in Germany, Roepke's friend, Luigi Einaudi, Italy's first president after the war, restored the Italian economy by implementing the measures advocated by Roepke.

In *A Humane Economy,* Roepke sets forth clearly and cogently the case for free-market capitalism. He rejects socialism as "a philosophy which...places too little emphasis on man, his nature, and his personality." With their fundamental misunderstanding of human nature, he argues, socialist regimes and collectivist economies are inherently repressive. In contrast, he defends the "intrinsic morality of the market economy," which allows the individual to profit by working for his own welfare and that of his fellow man. Roepke reveals himself as a philosopher as well as an economist with his description of economics as "a moral science," insisting that calculations and equations can never yield the sum of all things.

Writing at the height of the Cold War, Roepke predicted that the decisive battle between Communism and the free world would be fought on "the field of spiritual and moral values." Political leaders such as Ronald Reagan and Margaret Thatcher acted on this profound insight and ended the protracted conflict between the free world and the Communist world, not on the battlefield, but at the bargaining table. *A Humane Economy* is an uplifting free-market manifesto that did much to reverse the troubling trend toward economic collectivization after the Second World War.

Ethnic America: A History, Thomas Sowell (1981)

Why have the different ethnic groups of America—Irish, German, Jewish, Japanese, African-American, Mexican—reacted so differently to the American experience? Thomas Sowell, noted economist and arguably the most distinguished black intellectual in America, sets out to answer this critical question in *Ethnic America*. Each group, Sowell discovered in his research, was influenced by several factors: the ages of the immigrants, where they located in America, the date of their arrival, and the skills and cultures they brought with them. Immigrants living in the same neighborhoods and subjected to the same conditions did not turn out the same. Irish millionaires differed from Jewish millionaires. Black athletes dominated in some sports, Hispanics in others. Nobel Prize winners from different ethnic groups were successful in different sciences. However, Sowell says, the American experience has changed each group, and each group, in turn, has changed the American landscape.

The most dramatic example of change, Sowell writes, is the people sitting in Congress and on the Supreme Court whose ancestors were brought to America as slaves. Among the world's leading scientific, political, and economics figures are Americans whose immigrant ancestors were once dismissed as "the beaten men of beaten races." Jews rose faster than other groups because they seized upon free schools and libraries with "a tenacity and determination" seldom approached by others.

Blacks, Sowell says, are an exceptional group because they are the only ethnic group brought to America against their will. Black Americans are among the oldest Americans and also among the newest: They entered the larger society only after emancipation in 1863, and they arrived in urban America only with World War II. In that sense, Sowell says, "blacks are about where the Irish were one hundred years earlier." Nevertheless, blacks have moved from a position of "utter destitution" in money, knowledge, and rights to a place alongside other groups engaged in "the great struggles of life." No other group, Sowell states, has "had to come from so far back to join their fellow Americans."

In our individualistic society, Sowell writes, ethnic history reminds us of the "enduring consequences of centuries-old cultural patterns." It demonstrates how hard it is for differing groups and fragmented elements within those groups to get along with each other. But that history, objectively presented in *Ethnic America*, also shows that progress is possible for almost everyone, regardless of his ethnic background, in a society that is a unique mixture of unity, diversity, and opportunity.

Wealth and Poverty, George Gilder (1981)

In 1978, two of America's most prominent economists, Robert L. Heilbroner and John Kenneth Galbraith, declared that the main problems with the faltering American economy, mired in "stagflation," were that taxes were too low and regulations too few. Republican presidential candidate Ronald Reagan vehemently disagreed, insisting that if you reduced tax rates and allowed people to spend or save more of what they earned, they would "add fuel to the great economic machine that energizes our national progress." President Reagan's first major economic decision was to cut all income tax rates by 25 percent and index tax rates in order to offset the impact of inflation. Some analysts called this approach "supply-side economics." Reagan called it common sense. Many economists now agree that the Reagan tax cuts produced almost uninterrupted economic growth in America for the next quarter of a century.

Jude Wanniski in 1978 wrote the first book devoted to supply-side economics—*The Way the World Works*—but it is George Gilder in *Wealth and Poverty* who illuminates the social, political, and economic grounding of this school of economic thought. The true source of wealth, Gilder argues, is not natural resources or industrial production but "non-material forces" such as creativity, new technology, and the willingness to explore new territory. Capitalism, he says, is based not on greed but on giving. The true capitalist is an entrepreneur who invests his money and energy not knowing what his return will be.

As one reviewer remarked, George Gilder is part Charles Murray, part Ronald Reagan, and part Arthur C. Clarke. He dismisses the controlling economic policies of the Left, offering instead a quintessentially American vision of a free economy and a prosperous society resting on the pillars of "work, family and faith interdependently reaching toward…[the] future."

The Seven Fat Years: And How To Do It Again, Robert L. Bartley (1992)

Many liberal economists have characterized the 1980s as a "decade of greed," focusing solely on the savings and loan debacle and junk bond scams. But in those same years, America's gross national product grew by nearly one-third, Americans' standard of living increased by about one-fifth, the U.S. economy added 18.4 million jobs, and productivity rose by 10.6 percent. The "misery index"—the sum of the inflation and unemployment rates—peaked in 1980 and declined by nearly one-half by 1990. Far from being a time that benefited only the greedy and the rich, the 1980s constituted "seven fat years" for the majority of Americans.

In *The Seven Fat Years*, Robert L. Bartley, the late, great editor of *The Wall Street Journal*, skillfully shows how the severe economic crisis of the 1970s was overcome by policies put into place by President Ronald Reagan over the strong protests and dire warnings of a liberal establishment wed to Keynesian economics. Reagan's actions included a tight monetary policy and across-the-board tax cuts, which ignited a wave of American optimism and creativity. There was, among other advances, a communications revolution: In 1980, only 1 percent of American households owned a VCR, but by 1989, more than 58 percent did. The number of personal computers exploded from 2 million to 45 million.

An economy "is not an inanimate machine but a living organism," Bartley writes. Through his liberating policies and uplifting rhetoric, President Reagan led the way out of an economic wilderness and sparked "an economic expansion of unprecedented duration." The keys to growth, Bartley says, are to keep taxes low, keep spending under *some* control, maintain a stable currency, keep markets open, seek free exchange around the world, and let entrepreneurs compete. These actions constitute a winning formula in any decade.

The Mystery of Capital: Why Capitalism Triumphs in the West and Fails Everywhere Else, Hernando de Soto (2000)

While capitalism produces wealth and prosperity for most in the West, it is not working so well in much of the rest of the world. Is the reason because the West is more democratic and entrepreneurial? Or is it that the West has the necessary assets to make capitalism succeed and Western workers work harder and longer than those in the Third World? Or is the true reason that the West has a legal system that enables entrepreneurs of every size and shape to use their wealth—and the developing world does not?

Hernando de Soto, the noted Peruvian economist, argues in *The Mystery of Capital* that most poor countries do not have a structure of law that guarantees private property and encourages enterprise. Without such a legal foundation, they are unable to leverage property into wealth and create healthy free markets. According to de Soto, the total value of the real estate held but not legally owned by the poor of the Third World and former Communist nations is at least $9.3 trillion. If people of the Third World could mortgage a house for a new venture or publicly trade stock in a new company, de Soto argues, the economic impact would be startling. People would become more accountable, assets would become fungible, productive networks would be created, and transactions would be protected.

Importing McDonald's and Starbucks franchises, de Soto says, is not the way to create wealth in the underdeveloped world. "What is needed is capital, and this requires a complex and mighty system of legal property" that the West has taken for granted and the Third World has never known.

The Spirit of Democratic Capitalism, Michael Novak (1982)

Michael Novak once wrote that there is nothing more difficult for an intellectual of the Left than to engage his colleagues in criticism, for the certain punishment is excommunication. Nevertheless, Novak, long one of America's most prominent socialists, broke publicly with his leftist colleagues, declaring that "Socialism makes no sense as an economic theory" and had resulted in tyranny and poverty in almost all of the countries in which it had been tried. He compounded his "heresy" by embracing capitalism, which alone recognizes that "the cause of the wealth of nations is the creativity of the human person." Since his conversion to the Right in the late 1970s, Michael Novak has written book after book about economics, philosophy, politics, and culture; but his most important work, for which he received the prestigious Templeton Prize, is *The Spirit of Democratic Capitalism.*

In his innovative study, Novak, long associated with the American Enterprise Institute, describes the three dynamic and converging systems upon which democratic capitalism is based: a democratic polity, a market economy, and a moral culture. He argues that the natural logic of capitalism, with its emphasis on the individual, leads to democracy; that is, economic liberty and political liberty reinforce each other. Novak further asserts that democracy and the market economy require a moral social system. Democratic capitalism, Novak writes, is "not just a system but a way of life." Its ethos includes pluralism, a respect for unintended consequences, a sense of right and wrong, and a new conception of community, the individual, and the family.

As few writers before him have been able to do, Michael Novak helps us to understand the uniqueness of American democratic capitalism and why it has been able to revolutionize the ordinary expectations of human life.

STATESMANSHIP

$\mathcal{B}$elieving that men make history, not the reverse, we offer in the category of STATESMANSHIP the biographies of nine remarkable individuals, including Presidents George Washington, Abraham Lincoln, Harry Truman, and Ronald Reagan and two British politicians who profoundly affected American history and conservatism—Edmund Burke and Winston Churchill.

George Washington: The Indispensable Man,
James Thomas Flexner (1974)

It is impossible to fathom the achievement of the American Founding without recognizing the overwhelming significance of one man. Consider that for 21 years—from the moment he became commander in chief of continental forces in 1775 until his presidential retirement in 1796—George Washington was the *de facto* leader of the American struggle for independence, constitutional reform, and the establishment of the new nation. As military leader, chairman of the Constitutional Convention, and first President of the United States, Washington was at every important intersection of the Founding. His decisions and practical wisdom were crucial to its outcome at every stage. By comparison, Lincoln's national public life was intense but brief, spanning only seven years.

Such a life can be grasped only in the fullness of biography, showing the statesman grappling with all the contingencies and circumstances of a long life of action. James Thomas Flexner was an historian of the old school who believed that history was about what actually happened and that actual history reveals great individuals better than mythical stories or psychological profiling ever can. Already an historian of early American painting, Flexner spent seven years writing what is now considered the classic multi-volume biography of Washington, for which he received a special Pulitzer Prize citation. He distilled what he had learned into this one-volume biography, which tightly covers all the important events and captures the essence of Washington's exceptional character and unique life.

"To find again the ideals we have lost," Flexner writes, "we may not return to our national beginnings with the blinded eyes of idolatry or chauvinism. Let us determine without prejudice exactly what happened, exactly how men behaved. If we do this, we shall, so I am profoundly convinced, find, in the dark valley where we stand, inspiration."

Abraham Lincoln: A Biography, Benjamin P. Thomas (1952)

The incredible thing about Abraham Lincoln is that nearly all of the stories about him are true. He was born in a Kentucky log cabin and was the product of the American frontier. He taught himself to read from Parson Weems's *Life of Washington* and Grimshaw's *History of the United States;* his formal schooling totaled one year. He always had a zest for politics and first ran for public office in his early twenties. He made his first public disavowal of slavery at 28.

In 1858, Lincoln ran for the U.S. Senate from Illinois and narrowly lost to incumbent Democrat Stephen Douglas after besting his opponent in a series of debates. Following an eloquent speech on slavery at Cooper Union in New York, he was nominated by the new Republican Party to be its presidential candidate. He narrowly won the popular vote over Douglas but had a comfortable margin in the electoral college. Over the next four years, the former country lawyer made some of the most memorable addresses in American history and preserved the Union through the successful prosecution of a bloody civil war. His policies placed slavery on "the road to ultimate extinction," culminating in the Emancipation Proclamation. Five days after Lee surrendered to Grant at Appomattox, Lincoln was assassinated by a deranged actor while attending a play at Ford's Theatre.

Among the very best of the thousands of Lincoln books is Benjamin Thomas's biography, by virtue of its vivid writing, scrupulous research, and considered judgments. A masterful storyteller, Thomas brings Lincoln and his times to vibrant life. He concludes that the martyred President embodied, as few leaders have, America's fundamental principles of liberty and equality.

Man of the People: A Life of Harry S. Truman, Alonzo L. Hamby (1995)

Although Harry Truman left the presidency in 1953 widely discredited, by the 1990s he was ranked by the general public and most scholars as among the top Presidents in American history. Barry Goldwater admired him, and Ronald Reagan campaigned for him in Truman's 1948 "upset" victory. In *Man of the People*, noted liberal historian Alonzo Hamby offers a richly detailed character study that explains Truman's popular and scholarly standing. He was a plain-speaking President who put a sign reading "The Buck Stops Here" on his desk. He was a key architect of the policy of containment, encapsulated in the Truman Doctrine, the Marshall Plan, and

NATO, that kept the Soviet Union from bringing Western Europe and other parts of the free world into its sphere of influence. Of the latter accomplishment, Winston Churchill remarked to Truman, "You, more than any other man, have saved Western Civilization."

Truman was a man of paradoxes: personally honest but a product of the thoroughly corrupt Pendergast machine in Missouri; a firm believer in bipartisan foreign policy but a fierce partisan in domestic policy; a devout Christian who authorized the use of the atomic bomb—in Hamby's words, "the most awesome and indiscriminate weapon in human history." Truman said he never lost a night's sleep over his decision because it saved the lives of countless American servicemen poised to invade an intractable Japan bent on wholesale kamikaze.

David McCullough wrote a deservedly popular biography of Truman, but we recommend Hamby's *Man of the People* because it is more balanced in its discussion of Truman's strengths and weaknesses and more nuanced in its conclusions. Although unimpressive in appearance and a poor speaker, Truman became an icon, Hamby says, because most Americans see Truman "as an ordinary man" who fought for their interests, made great decisions, and demonstrated their potential.

Governor Reagan: His Rise to Power, Lou Cannon (2003)

Before there was President Reagan, there was Governor Reagan, whose eight-year tenure as California's chief executive foretold his performance as the most significant President of the second half of the 20th century. The Reagan administration in Sacramento from 1967 to 1974 spanned a time of unprecedented inflation and two recessions, civil unrest over the Vietnam War and frequent campus uprisings, violence in the inner cities, and the Watergate scandal. In the midst of this turbulent political atmosphere, Governor Reagan pursued a policy of "squeeze, cut and trim" that kept California's taxes and spending from soaring into the stratosphere. He made first-class appointments to the bench and set a high moral standard for public life. He pioneered a welfare reform that emerged as a central issue in national politics.

In *Governor Reagan*, former *Washington Post* reporter Lou Cannon offers a perceptive and gracefully written account of the gubernatorial years, as well as a brief description of Reagan's early years in radio and Hollywood, his almost successful run for the Republican presidential nomination in 1976, and his 1980 victory over President Jimmy Carter. Cannon knows Reagan as well as he knows politics, and the result is an outstanding political biography.

Although a near political novice, Cannon writes, Reagan mastered the intricacies of governing "the nation's most populous and macroscopic state." He proved, as no one had before him, that it was possible to succeed as governor of a major state without abandoning conservative principles. Reagan carried his doctrine of limited government to the national political level from which, Cannon writes, "he tugged the nation in a conservative direction."

Churchill: A Life, Martin Gilbert (1991)

Every child has a hero—someone who inspires by his or her words and deeds. Nations also have heroes who shine the brightest during times of darkness. Ronald Reagan reinvigorated America with his strong leadership and unswerving dedication to conservative ideas, but who inspired Reagan? In a 1990 address, the former President invoked the indomitable spirit of Winston Churchill during World War II. He recalled that when Churchill became prime minister in 1939, France had fallen to Nazi Germany and Britain faced the threat of imminent invasion. Churchill navigated his imperiled country through the storm with confidence, bravery, and unmatched rhetorical skill.

In *Churchill: A Life*, Sir Martin Gilbert, Churchill's official biographer, chronicles the 90 turbulent years of the British statesman who received his Army commission during the reign of Queen Victoria and at the age of 76 was elected prime minister for the second time. Gilbert's authoritative biography of nearly 1,000 pages is based on four decades of research and writing about the man many consider *the* public figure of the 20th century.

Churchill was a member of both the Liberal and Conservative parties during his 55 years in Parliament and often supported social reform, including the National Health Service. However, in the 1950 election won by Conservatives, Churchill declared that the choice before the voters was "to take another plunge into socialist regimentation" or "regain the freedom, initiative, and opportunity of British life." His finest hour, Gilbert argues convincingly, "was the leadership of Britain [in 1940] when it was most isolated, most threatened, and most weak; when his own courage, determination, and belief in democracy became at one with the nation."

In addition to his political accomplishments, Churchill was a prolific and popular writer: The first volume of his award-winning history *The Second World War*, for example, is discussed on page 93 of this *Guide*.

Goldwater: The Man Who Made a Revolution, Lee Edwards (1995)

While many conservatives—philosophers, popularizers, and politicians—have played important parts in the rise of the Right, one man in particular ignited the conservative revolution. This politician first raised the domestic and foreign policy issues—the tyranny of intrusive government, the corruption brought on by welfare, the danger of appeasing totalitarians—that have dominated the national debate for half a century. As a presidential candidate, he inspired a generation of young men and women to commit themselves to mastering the political process and making conservatism a consequential political force in America.

As Lee Edwards recounts in his dramatic biography that often reads like a novel, Barry Goldwater was an unlikely revolutionary. He was the grandson of a Jewish peddler who became a millionaire. He was a college dropout whose manifesto, *The Conscience of a Conservative* (see page 17) sold over 3 million copies. He was a gifted photographer whose sensitive portraits of Native Americans and scenes of Arizona hung in galleries around the world. He was an intrepid pilot who flew more than 170 different planes, including the U-2 and the latest jets. He delighted in challenging unconventional wisdom but always used the principles of the Constitution and American Founding as his guide.

Goldwater was the most consequential presidential loser in American politics. In 1994, almost 30 years to the day after President Lyndon B. Johnson roundly defeated him, a national poll found that 64 percent of Americans agreed with the Republicans' Contract with America. The people wanted a less expansive welfare state, lower taxes and spending, tougher anti-crime measures, and less Washington meddling in their lives. Every one of these ideas, Edwards points out, was first proposed by Goldwater in his 1964 campaign. He was simply 30 years too early.

Goldwater's candidacy for President marked the beginning of a dramatic shift in American politics—from East to West, from the cities to the suburbs, from containment to liberation, from liberal to conservative—that continues to this day.

American Caesar: Douglas MacArthur 1880–1964,
William Manchester (1978)

Douglas MacArthur was one of America's greatest military commanders, a general who led troops into no-man's land during World War I and island-hopped his way to Japan during World War II, often wading ashore just hours after the first wave of U.S. forces. At the age of 70, he commanded the daring Inchon landing that freed all of South Korea from Communist domination. *American Caesar* is a telling portrayal of a complex man-at-arms with a soaring intellect and a will of iron who was either worshiped or despised by those who served under him.

MacArthur is often derided as a reactionary and relic of the 19th century; but as distinguished historian William Manchester explains, MacArthur was frequently an agent of change—and for the better. He reformed the military academy at West Point, bringing it into the 20th century. His campaign against Japan rewrote the book on how to defeat an enemy without confronting him directly. His total casualties in the South Pacific from Australia to V-J Day were fewer than Eisenhower's in the Battle of the Bulge alone. During his years as American viceroy in Japan after the war, MacArthur introduced the Japanese to civil liberties, labor unions, equal rights for women, and land reform.

No other commander has been more controversial. When MacArthur advocated expanding the Korean War beyond the Administration's policy, President Truman relieved him of his command. On the other hand, George Marshall, who intensely disliked him personally, acknowledged that MacArthur was "our most brilliant general." *American Caesar* is an irresistible read and biography at its best. Asked to explain the secret of Manchester's prose, the eminent critic Clifton Fadiman commented, "Its supreme value can be stated simply: *you are there.*"

Narrative of the Life of Frederick Douglass, An American Slave, Written by Himself, Introduction by Henry Louis Gates, Jr. (1997)

Only in America could a slave become one of the country's most remarkable statesmen. Born a slave, Frederick Douglass taught himself to read and write, survived the brutality of slave-owners, and grew into a man who could only, to paraphrase an American Revolution motto, "live free or die." By reason of his eloquence in print and on the speaker's platform, Douglass was the nation's most prominent black abolitionist prior to the Civil War.

In *Narrative of the Life of Frederick Douglass, An American Slave* (first published in 1845), the author recounts how he learned to read after overhearing his master say about him: "If you teach [him] how to read…it would forever unfit him to be a slave." The master was correct: Reading led to writing—and finally to Douglass's resolution to liberate himself from slavery through literacy. An instant best-seller, the narrative recounts the cruel whippings and murders of helpless slaves and their failed escapes. The book ends with Douglass resolving to fight a "nigger-breaker" rather than submit to another beating. Although he would remain a slave for another four years, the battle was a turning point in his life, reviving self-confidence and a "sense of [my] own manhood." The encounter, he writes, "was a glorious resurrection, from the tomb of slavery to the heaven of freedom."

Tall and handsome and with a rich, melodious voice, Douglass became one of the best-known orators in America, an adviser to President Lincoln, and the first black man to be invited to the White House. He was, in the words of Harvard professor Henry L. Gates, Jr., America's first black "public intellectual." One hundred and sixty years after its publication,

Narrative of the Life of Frederick Douglass remains an American classic and a testimony to man's innate desire to be free.

RELIGION

"*R*eligion in America," wrote Alexis de Tocqueville in the 1830s, "takes no direct part in the government of society, but it must be regarded as the first of their political institutions." So it was, and so it is today. Despite the American Civil Liberties Union and similar groups devoted to the separation of church and state, religion plays a critical role in the public debate over controversial political issues such as abortion, school prayer, and same-sex marriage. More broadly, religion is critical in shaping the morals and character that are necessary for liberty and republican government.

In the RELIGION category, we offer nine far-ranging books, from a history of religion in America and a biography of Pope John Paul II to a look at "the two faces" of Islam.

Mere Christianity, C. S. Lewis (1943)

No Christian writer left a greater mark on the 20th century than C. S. Lewis. Much of his enormous popularity—his works continue to sell in the hundreds of thousands annually—can be traced to *Mere Christianity.*

The book's enormous appeal lies in the ability of its author, an Oxford-educated English scholar who taught Medieval and Renaissance literature at Cambridge and Oxford, to outline the basic tenets of Christianity in a language any layman can grasp. He strives to draw a line, not between denominations but between believers and non-believers, by explaining the logic and the reasonableness behind what all Christians hold to be true.

Lewis, a middle-aged convert to the Church of England, was well-suited to the task. He makes one thing plain from the start of the book (adapted from a series of radio addresses): There is a basic standard of behavior that all people accept, whether they realize it or not, and all fall short of it. From there, he embarks on a candid examination of core Christian beliefs and practices as he builds to the central point of his work: All of us are challenged to make a decision about the claims of Jesus Christ. Neutrality is not possible, Lewis says. Either He is who He said He was or He was a lunatic.

The Church, according to Lewis, exists solely "to draw men to Christ—to make them little Christs. If they are not doing that, cathedrals, missions, sermons, even the Bible itself, are a waste of time." Lewis, with his clear writing style and airtight logic, makes the Church's job much easier. This Christian classic still enjoys almost universal popularity some six decades after its publication and 40 years after Lewis's death.

Orthodoxy, G. K. Chesterton (1908)

A fundamental conservative belief is that society should alter slowly, but what happens when society is plunged into a bloody conflict and undergoes an economic sea change as occurred at the beginning of the 20th century—and as is happening in the early years of the 21st century? How does a conservative, or anyone, survive in a time of revolution and radicalism?

Searching for an answer almost a century ago, noted British writer G. K. Chesterton—a former agnostic who converted to the Anglican Church and then to Catholicism—

rejected the anarchist and materialist beliefs fashionable among the intelligentsia of the day. "How can we contrive to be at once astonished by the world," he asked, "and yet be at home in it?" His answer was that we must place our trust in our intellectual inheritance and sacred traditions. Indeed, he said, it is only through a conservative worldview that humanity can retain its sanity.

In *Orthodoxy*, Chesterton offers an ethical system based on four principles: astonishment at the possibilities of life, gratitude for life itself, joy in constancy, and dedication to restraint. Providing a foundation for this system is the Christian (Catholic) Church, which he likens to a heavenly chariot that flies through the ages leaving "the dull heresies sprawling and prostrate" and "the wild truth reeling but erect."

Orthodoxy is a companion book to the author's earlier *Heretics* and is vintage Chesterton. It is witty, profound, and filled with glittering epigrams such as, "It is always easy to let the age have its head; the difficult thing is to keep one's own." Conservatives such as C. S. Lewis and William F. Buckley Jr. have acknowledged their literary and religious debt to G. K. Chesterton, the "prince of paradox" and a defender of the Christian faith against a hostile world.

Here I Stand: A Life of Martin Luther, Roland H. Bainton (1950)

In 1505, a 22-year-old university student and devout Catholic was knocked to the ground by a lightning bolt and cried out in terror, "St. Anne, help me! I will become a monk." Before he died four decades later, Martin Luther had repudiated the "cult" of saints, renounced monasticism, shattered the mighty structure of Medieval Catholicism, and ignited the Protestant Reformation. So begins Ronald

Bainton's biography of one of the most influential religious figures of Western civilization.

Reformation scholar Bainton draws the reader into the life of Martin Luther and the 16th century through the great reformer's sermons, letters, and debates and the use of more than 100 woodcuts and engravings from the time. The author is prudential in his depiction of Luther, steering between his followers, who hailed him as a prophet and deliverer of Germany, and his opponents, who called him a heretic and destroyer of Christendom. Bainton offers a vivid portrait of Luther as a passionate individualist, detailing his flaws and faults as well as his unshakable faith in the Word of God.

Bainton suggests that no one did more to fashion the character of the German people than Martin Luther, particularly through his translation of the Bible into German. Lutheranism, with its emphasis on the scriptures and justification by faith alone, remains strong in Germany and Scandinavia and has an extensive following in America. Luther's most significant contribution in the area of Christianity was his steadfast belief in the Bible as the sole rule of faith. "The true Christian pilgrimage," he said, "is not to Rome...but to the...Gospels."

The Old Religion in a New World: The History of North American Christianity, Mark A. Noll (2002)

"The spirit of religion and the spirit of freedom...[are] united intimately with one another" in America, wrote Alexis de Tocqueville. Indeed, from the birth of the Republic, there was an intermingling of Christian belief and political thought that shaped the way Americans thought about themselves and their country. Was there something "new" in the Christian religion practiced on this continent as compared with the "old" religion in Europe? Award-winning church historian Mark Noll identifies four special factors in North American

Christianity: the almost unlimited physical space, racial and ethnic diversity, religious pluralism, and firm convictions regarding freedom.

Noll combines a chronological history of North American religion from the late 15th century to the present with essays about the separation of church and state and the political involvement of the churches in events such as the Cold War and the civil rights movement. At the start of the 21st century, Noll predicts, the following trends will shape the Christian faith in America: The number of Roman Catholics, led by Hispanics, will rise; "free-flowing Pentecostal and charismatic styles" will spread their influence; and the most important Christian schisms will follow theological and ideological rather than denominational lines. The result, says Noll, will be "even further erosion of the importance of denominations" in American Christian life.

The Old Religion in a New World shows how the American experience has changed the churches but not the essential faith of America.

Protestant–Catholic–Jew: An Essay in American Religious Sociology, Will Herberg (1955)

Just as Tocqueville's *Democracy in America* is a vital guide to understanding the American spirit in the mid-19th century, so Will Herberg's *Protestant–Catholic–Jew* provides a telling portrait of the "American way of life" in the mid-20th century. Americans in Tocqueville's era held their religion "to be indispensable to the maintenance of republican institutions." A century later, Herberg wrote that American religion and society are so closely interrelated "as to make it virtually impossible to understand either without reference to the other."

Herberg dismisses the image of America as a giant melting pot. Rather, he says, the nation is more accurately conceived as one great community divided along religious lines into three sub-communities: Protestant, Catholic, and Jewish. These three religious groups are diverse representations of similar spiritual values centered on a belief in God and similar political values centered on a commitment to representative democracy. The American way of life, Herberg says, is individualistic, pragmatic, and moralistic; it is the "common faith of the American people."

Described by the eminent theologian Reinhold Niebuhr as "the most fascinating essay on the religious sociology of America" when it was published, *Protestant–Catholic–Jew* is not without its flaws. It fails to anticipate adequately, for example, the future theological split between mainline and evangelical Protestants. But its analysis anticipates and explains the modern conservative coalition of fundamentalist Protestants, Roman Catholics, and orthodox Jews on such social issues as abortion.

The Naked Public Square: Religion and Democracy in America, Richard John Neuhaus (1984)

With the emergence of activist groups like the Moral Majority in the late 1970s and their major impact on the presidential campaign in 1980, alarmed secularists warned that participation by the Religious Right threatened the American "tradition" of excluding religion from the conduct of public business. Based on an expansive view of the separation of church and state, the secularists argued, the public square should and must be "naked"—that is, devoid of religiously grounded values.

Not so, responded the prominent Lutheran minister Richard John Neuhaus, who called the idea of America as a secular society not only "demonstrably false," but "exceedingly dangerous." The values of the American people, he stated, "are deeply rooted in religion."

In *The Naked Public Square*, Neuhaus points out that the struggle for American independence in the 18th century, the abolition of slavery in the 19th century, and the civil rights movement in the 20th century were all motivated by religious forces. In addressing the issues of school prayer and abortion in the 1960s and 1970s, the author says, Christian activists were not acting in violation of the Constitution but responding to the reality that politics is a function of culture and "at the heart of [America's] culture is religion." The public sphere, insists Neuhaus, now a Catholic priest, cannot be naked. Only religion can provide the morality necessary for the success of the American experiment.

A Rumor of Angels: Modern Society and the Rediscovery of the Supernatural, Peter L. Berger (1969)

Reflecting the revolutionary mood of the 1960s, many intellectuals of the Left, paraphrasing Nietzsche, proclaimed that God was dead and we were living in a post-Christian era. The supernatural had departed from the modern world, never to return, they said—with unrestrained satisfaction. Peter Berger, an émigré and long-time professor of sociology and theology at Boston University, offered a ringing response, arguing that there is a transcendent dimension of life in nearly all societies.

In *A Rumor of Angels*, he lists five "signals of transcendence": man's propensity for order, his joyful play as child and adult, his hope for the future, his belief in damnation, and his sense of humor. Religion, Berger writes, is not only a projection of human order, but also, from the view of what he calls "inductive faith," the "ultimately true vindication of order." Man's ability to hope, despite the reality of suffering and death, suggests the transcendent. As a case in point, he says, there are certain deeds, such as the Nazi Holocaust, that cry out for eternal punishment and damnation. A prototypical manifestation of the comic in Western literature, he writes, is Don Quixote, who represents the truth that the idealist is often wiser than the realist.

Berger proposes "a rediscovery of the supernatural" based on inductive faith. This will have political as well as moral consequences, he says, for the principal benefit of religion is that it permits confrontation with the age in which one lives and both "vindicates courage and safeguards against fanaticism." Written for a general audience, *A Rumor of Angels* is an articulate defense of religious faith that is as pertinent today as when it was written nearly four decades ago.

The Two Faces of Islam: The House of Sa'ud from Tradition to Terror, Stephen Schwartz (2002)

In the wake of September 11, 2001, some Americans suspected there was something inherently militant, even evil, in Islam that made the terrorist attacks inevitable. Not so, declares author and journalist Stephen Schwartz, who says that terrorism is at odds with true Islam. Instead, he blames an extremist ideology known as Wahhabism, a "death cult" that is the official religion of Saudi Arabia. According to Schwartz, the Saudis have spent decades and billions of dollars exporting Wahhabism to the rest of the world, from Pakistan to the United States. To avoid a clash of civilizations, Schwartz says, there must be a "meaningful effort" to counterpose traditional Islam—pluralistic and peaceful—to Wahhabi–Saudi extremism and its promotion of terror.

In *The Two Faces of Islam*, Schwartz recounts briefly the history of Islam, beginning with the birth of the prophet Muhammad in 570 in the city of Mecca in what is now Saudi

Arabia. He describes 1,000 years of Islamic expansion throughout Europe and Asia. Wahhabism was founded in 1703 in the central Arabian region of Najd. The Wahhabis reconquered Mecca in the 1920s and, with the discovery of oil in Arabia in the 1930s, became "the world's richest and most powerful ruling elite." With the collapse of the Soviet Union in 1991, writes Schwartz, Wahhabism replaced Communism as the main sponsor of international aggression against the democratic West. Osama bin Laden, he says, is the 21st century Wahhabi hero "par excellence."

In the last chapter, Schwartz suggests how to bring about an end to the Saudi monarchy and to reach out to traditional Muslims in Turkey, the Balkans, Malaysia, and other countries. The fall of Wahhabism, Schwartz says, would foster new relations among all monotheistic believers—Jews, Christians, and Muslims—and lead to an appreciation of their commonalities rather than an emphasis on their differences. Readers of *The Two Faces of Islam* will come away with a better understanding of a major world religion and its various practitioners.

Witness to Hope: The Biography of Pope John Paul II, George Weigel (1999)

Since Jesus Christ called the apostle Peter the "rock" on which he would build his church nearly 2,000 years ago, 265 men have served as head of the Catholic Church, the world's largest Christian denomination. Among them have been many saints and a few scoundrels, some mystics and quite a few politicians, the memorable and the forgettable, but only a few have been given the title of "Great." In his monumental biography *Witness to Hope*, the distinguished Catholic author George Weigel asserts that John Paul II (Karol Wojtyla of Poland) deserves the name "John Paul the Great."

Weigel rejects the thesis that John Paul II's papacy was basically "political," as reflected in his support of the Solidarity movement in Poland and other anti-Communist efforts in Eastern Europe. Nor does he accept that John Paul II was simply a prophet of nonviolence à la Gandhi or Martin Luther King. Rather, the author argues that the Pope was a passionate apostle of Christian humanism, viewing his mission as that of a witness to the truth about the salvific relationship between God and Man. Weigel describes how, among his many accomplishments, John Paul II revitalized the papacy through constant pilgrimages throughout the world (traveling 2.8 times the distance between the Earth and the moon); redefined the Church's ecumenical relationship with Judaism and met frequently with Orthodox and Protestant leaders; and was responsible for, along with his 13 encyclicals and numerous other writings, the *Catechism of the Catholic Church*, the church's first official instructional document in more than 400 years.

Witness to Hope is an historical, philosophical, and theological *tour de force* that is worthy, as Harvard Law professor Mary Ann Glendon puts it, "of the man of the century."

AMERICAN
HISTORY

*A*ll of American history is a miracle—not just the writing of the sublime Constitution in five months. It is the story of the triumph of extraordinary and ordinary men and women over an untamed wilderness, British might, a bloody Civil War, a Great Depression, two world wars, Nazism, Communism, racism, and the seductions of the welfare state. "No other national story holds such tremendous lessons," historian Paul Johnson has written, "for the American people themselves and for the rest of mankind." Those who wish to conserve America and its principles must have a deep understanding of this story.

The 12 titles in the category of AMERICAN HISTORY span the nation's 400 years, from David Hackett Fisher's recounting of the first English settlers to Stephen Hayward's *The Age of Reagan*.

The Birth of the Republic, 1763–89,
Edmund S. Morgan (1956)

Edmund Morgan's short political history of the founding of the American Republic has been a favorite of college students for generations because it is clear and lively in its language, is fair and balanced in its treatment of both the American and British sides, and shows, in 156 pages, how 13 contentious colonies transformed themselves into a unified nation. The initial causes were arbitrary British taxation and an imperious Parliament; the final responses were a Declaration of Independence and a new Constitution for a new nation. The reader is caught up in a vivid and often suspenseful narrative with all the makings of an epic story. How could so small and scattered a country defeat the most powerful military power on Earth? How would the diverse delegates assembled in Philadelphia reconcile their considerable differences and write a Constitution for a new nation and for all time?

The theme of *The Birth of the Republic*, the author explains, is the search by these early Americans for the principles on which they could take a common stand. In their search, they discovered that the core principle of human equality "would turn the course of history in a new direction" and affect the course of human events to this day.

Along with Morgan's sure-handed depiction of the nation's birth, the 1977 edition of *The Birth of the Republic* contains the texts of the Declaration of Independence, the Articles of Confederation, and the Constitution and a bibliographic essay about other historical works concerning the Revolution and the Constitution. No one does a better job than Morgan of distilling the extraordinary story of how our nation was created.

Albion's Seed: Four British Folkways in America,
David Hackett Fischer (1989)

In a nation beset by general ignorance about its history, massive influxes of legal and illegal immigrants, and emotional clashes over cultural symbols, it is safe to say that America is going through something of an identity crisis. To the question of "Who are we?" cultural historian David Hackett Fischer answers that we are a European country settled and shaped by immigrants from four parts of England. First came the literate, austere Puritans who settled Massachusetts and present-day New England. The next to make inroads on the North American continent were the royalist cavaliers who established an agrarian society in Virginia and its environs. Then came the egalitarian Quakers who promoted a social pluralism in the Delaware Valley. The fourth group was the borderland English, Scots, and Irish who sought and found a better life in the American backcountry.

Fischer writes in *Albion's Seed* that the people of these four cultures shared certain characteristics: the English language, a respect for liberty under law, a Protestant Christian faith, and a belief in private property. When life, liberty, and property were threatened by the British King and Parliament, these four seemingly diverse yet complementary cultures joined together in the movement that led to the American Revolution. Despite the contemporary tendency toward secularism and multiculturalism, Fischer argues, the original four regions of British America continue to have a profound influence on America's culture and politics, especially in their idea of a "voluntary society" encouraged and protected by a culture of freedom.

Although *Albion's Seed* is almost 900 pages long, it is easily read because of Fischer's entertaining writing style and eye for the relevant detail. He points out, for example, that in colonial Virginia, a gentleman sheriff did not lay his hands on a felon; that was the work of his assistants. On the other hand, in a Quaker household, everyone dined together—parents, children, hired men, servants, and slaves alike. Only in colonial British America did one find unity in diversity, presaging the national motto of the United States, *"e pluribus unum"*—"out of many, one."

The Roots of American Order, Russell Kirk (1974)

Why do we Americans enjoy liberty, justice, and equality? From whence come our individual freedom, limited government, market economy, and core values? In *The Roots of American Order*, Russell Kirk argues that America is not only the land of the free and the home of the brave, but also a place of liberty that is fundamentally *ordered* in nature.

Using the device of five cities—Jerusalem, Athens, Rome, London, and Philadelphia—Kirk traces the roots of American order to a long-standing tradition in human history. First came the Hebrews, who recognized a "purposeful moral existence under God" and planted the seeds of the order nearly 3,000 years ago in Jerusalem. Next came the Greeks of Athens, who strengthened the order with their philosophical and political self-awareness. There followed the Romans, who nurtured it with their emphasis on law and social order. The order was intertwined with "the Christian understanding of human duties and human hopes" and joined by medieval custom, learning, and valor. The roots of order were further enriched by the political experiments in law and liberty that occurred in London, the mother of Parliaments, and Philadelphia, the birthplace of the American Republic's founding documents—the Declaration of Independence and the Constitution.

Throughout America's history, Kirk writes, technological innovations, massive population shifts, economic dislocations, political partisanship, an ever-present mass media, racial and ethnic tensions, and a virulent counterculture have shaken the nation; yet the general character of America has remained remarkably unaltered. In this far-ranging and illuminating book, intellectual historian Kirk describes the essential beliefs and institutions that anchor the polity we call the United States of America.

The Founders and the Classics: Greece, Rome, and the American Enlightenment, Carl J. Richard (1994)

Respected historians such as Clinton Rossiter and Bernard Bailyn have written that the classics did not exert a formative influence on the American Founding. Jefferson, Adams, Madison, and other authors of the Declaration of Independence and the Constitution, they claim, used the ancient Greeks and Romans as mere "window dressing." The Founders did not look to Aristotle, Cicero, or the Roman senate for guidance and inspiration in their writing and deliberations as much as they looked to Locke, Montesquieu, and the British Parliament. However, in *The Founders and the Classics*, the gifted young classics scholar Carl Richard argues that, in fact, classical Greece and Rome provided many of the Founders' intellectual tools.

Richard presents an arsenal of evidence to prove his thesis. Many of the Founders chose for their literary and journalistic pseudonyms names of classical figures whose challenges and situations mirrored his own. A young Thomas Jefferson copied into his commonplace book Tacitus's warning against the dangers of too many laws. In *The Federalist*, Hamilton warned of the fate of ancient republics, and Madison pointed out how the Spartan, Roman, and Carthaginian senates had acted as an "anchor against popular fluctuations," a potentially dangerous destabilizing force for the young American Republic. John Adams was perhaps the most ardent classicist among the Founders, pointing to the "great examples of Greece and Rome" when he enumerated the branches of knowledge that would illuminate the new nation's path.

Although written by an academic, *The Founders and the Classics* is neither pedantic nor ponderous. It is a particularly useful book for today's young conservatives because it confirms the Founders' direct indebtedness to the works of antiquity—a connection which, it is hoped, will encourage the reading of classics such as Plato's *The Republic* and Cato's speeches.

Constitutionalism: Ancient and Modern, Charles Howard McIlwain (1947)

Although the political leader of a nation that lacks a written constitution, British Prime Minister William Gladstone in 1878 described the U.S. Constitution as "the most wonderful work ever struck off at a given time by the brain and purpose of man." So powerful has been the American example that every country in the world, with the exception of Britain, New Zealand, and Israel, now has a written constitution. Much has been written about constitutional law and modern constitutional history, usually starting with the American and French Revolutions, but comparatively little attention has been paid to the origins of constitutionalism itself. More than 60 years ago, Pulitzer Prize–winning historian Charles Howard McIlwain wrote this definitive book, only 180 pages in length, which traces the development of constitutions from the Greeks and Romans to the present day.

In *Constitutionalism: Ancient and Modern*, McIlwain writes that it is not the Greeks (Plato described constitutional government as a "second best" system) but the Romans with their concept of a republican government who had the greatest influence on modern constitutionalism. He argues that the true essence of Roman constitutionalism lies in the principle that the people are "the ultimate source of legal authority." The fundamental weakness of medieval constitutionalism,

McIlwain says, lies in its failure to enforce any penalty against a prince who exceeded his legitimate authority.

It was incumbent on the writers of the U.S. Constitution to institute a revolutionary new principle: that a government "is only the creature of the constitution." Written constitutions that create, define, and limit governments, McIlwain says, are now the general rule in the world. The most successful constitutions and governments, he concludes, are those that follow the American example in which "will and law" are effectively balanced and liberty is thereby preserved.

Novus Ordo Seclorum: The Intellectual Origins of the Constitution, Forrest McDonald (1985)

If, as Catherine Drinker Bowen has written, the framing of the U.S. Constitution at the Philadelphia Convention in 1787 was a "miracle," what were the ideas that guided the miracle-workers? Were they primarily economic, ideological, or legal? Who were the thinkers that most influenced the Founders— Locke, Montesquieu, Blackstone, or Machiavelli? If we cannot answer these critical questions, if we do not know the true intellectual origins of the Constitution, we will be unable to resist the latest intellectual fads or defend our founding document against harmful interpretations and subversions.

Honored constitutional historian Forrest McDonald provides the answers in *Novus Ordo Seclorum*. McDonald asserts that, although the Framers drew upon a wide variety of philosophical and ideological sources—Locke for the idea of "the Laws of Nature and of Nature's God," Montesquieu for the idea of separation of powers—they relied upon their personal experience and common sense to construct "a new order for the ages." They were not armchair philosophers but political leaders. They were practical, prudent, and willing to compromise but also committed to the idea of, in Madison's words, "a government which derives all its powers directly or indirectly from the great body of the people."

A miracle the Constitution may well have been, but, as McDonald points out in his inestimable work, it was a miracle made by men who believed that the proper ends of government were to protect people in their lives, liberty, and property and that these ends could best be preserved through a republic.

Miracle at Philadelphia: The Story of the Constitutional Convention, May to September 1787, Catherine Drinker Bowen (1966)

Just four years after winning its independence from the greatest military power in the world, the new United States of America was in danger of splitting asunder. The war debt still loomed large. States and regions fought over boundaries and passed tariffs against each other. Nine states had their own navies. Massachusetts suffered public humiliation over Daniel Shays's farmer rebellion. Britain and Spain eyed America's vast territories covetously. The leaders of the infant republic saw that the Articles of Confederation were not working and needed mending and even replacement. And so, in the summer of 1787, 55 delegates from the 13 states convened in Philadelphia and in five months produced the U.S. Constitution, the most enduring of political documents.

In *Miracle at Philadelphia*, esteemed biographer Catherine Drinker Bowen captures the tensions and rivalries of the Convention and the contrasting personalities of Washington, Hamilton, Franklin, and Madison. Of the latter, she says, "no one came better prepared intellectually" for the formidable challenges of the undertaking. Bowen weaves a compelling story of the heated debates about the Virginia Plan, representation in the Senate, and the Great Compromise over slavery. An open admirer of the Convention and its delegates, Bowen argues that those assembled understood how much was at stake and labored night and day to create a new government consistent with the ideals of the Republic and "acceptable to the people" as well.

The author's vivid recreation of the Constitutional Convention and the succeeding fight for ratification among the states makes *Miracle at Philadelphia* recommended reading for anyone who wants to understand the stormy formative years of our nation.

Crisis of the House Divided: An Interpretation of the Issues in the Lincoln–Douglas Debates, Harry V. Jaffa (1959)

Many scholars argue that the most important debates in American political history were those between Abraham Lincoln and Stephen Douglas in 1858. The central issue was slavery, the corrosive force that brought about the Civil War, the bloodiest and costliest conflict in our history. The debates made the previously unknown Lincoln a national figure and enabled him to win the presidency only two years later. During the debates, Lincoln, more than any other politician of his time, upheld the Declaration of Independence and the idea that "all men are created equal" as indispensable to the American ethic and system of governance. These are the essential themes of Harry Jaffa's *Crisis of the House Divided*, written in large part to refute revisionist historians who asserted that there were no substantial differences between Lincoln and Douglas.

Jaffa contends that the doctrine of "popular sovereignty" as preached by Douglas was a parody of popular rights and implied that "rights" consisted merely of whatever public opinion deemed acceptable at the time, including slavery. Lincoln, Jaffa argues, offered a different and higher doctrine on which to build a polity: a moral sense that no man can rightfully achieve or retain his freedom "if he would deny to any other man" the equal right to equal freedom. Thus, he concludes, Lincoln provided the moral dimension missing from the Founding. However, as the academic Edward J. Erler points out in his more recent volume, *A New Birth of Freedom*, Jaffa concedes that the classical elements of prudence and natural law he once attributed exclusively to Lincoln's "refounding" were intrinsic to the Republic.

Like all of Jaffa's work, *Crisis of the House Divided* is scholarly and polemical, deeply philosophical and yet practical in its analysis. The book shows Lincoln to be a political thinker of the first class, confirming why he ranks second only to George Washington in the pantheon of American Presidents.

Battle Cry of Freedom: The Civil War Era, James M. McPherson (1988)

The Civil War is the most written-about event in American history, with an estimated 75,000 titles about the war and another 15,000 about its central political figure, Abraham Lincoln. Several multi-volume series tell about the conflict and its causes as well as the lives and careers of major military heroes such as Ulysses S. Grant and Robert E. Lee. And little wonder: More than 620,000 soldiers on both sides lost their lives in four years of conflict, as many as died in all of the nation's other wars combined, including Vietnam. Slavery was ended in the world's largest slaveholding country. The war transformed a federal *union* into a new *nation*. Six generations have passed, but the war is still fresh in the hearts and minds of many Americans. They visit Civil War battlefields, reenact battles, collect memorabilia, publish magazines, and demand still more books.

One work is widely accepted as the standard one-volume history of the Civil War: James McPherson's *Battle Cry of*

Freedom. McPherson, regarded as the leading authority on the American Civil War, offers a dramatic, integrated, and always accessible narrative of the tumultuous period, from the events that preceded secession through the end of the war. Everything is included: the publication of *Uncle Tom's Cabin*, the Dred Scott decision, the Lincoln–Douglas debates, the origins of the Republican Party, Lee's decision to lead the Confederate forces, the Emancipation Proclamation, Gettysburg, the terrible Wilderness campaign, Lincoln's reelection in 1864 despite a scurrilous press and propaganda campaign, and John Wilkes Booth's vow, following an April 11, 1965, speech by Lincoln on peace and Reconstruction, to make it "the last speech he will ever make."

Battle Cry of Freedom is a masterful chronicle of the great issues of the day—slavery, the structure of Northern and Southern society, the American economy, the competing nationalisms of the North and the South—and of the war that transformed America and produced, in Lincoln's words, a "new birth of freedom."

America: The Last Best Hope, Volume I: From the Age of Discovery to a World at War, William J. Bennett (2006)

In his Farewell Address to the American people, President Reagan warned, "If we forget what we did, we won't know who we are." Nevertheless, surveys continue to show that the magnitude of this country's accomplishments starting with the Founding is barely known to most Americans; they are too often subjected to dull, dumbed-down histories in school. While other books in this category show particular parts of our history to be enlightening and exciting, none of them offers an overall history of America. *America: The Last Best Hope* meets that need—and does so impressively.

In the first of two volumes, best-selling author and former U.S. Secretary of Education William J. Bennett offers a lively narrative of the triumphs and tragedies of America from the age of discovery to a world at war in 1914. He begins with the intrepid Columbus and follows with the early travails of the Pilgrims, who knew their mission into the North American wilderness to be of deep and lasting significance. He describes the pivotal gathering of the Constitutional Convention in Philadelphia in 1787 with a befitting appreciation of the political genius and wisdom of the Founders, remarking that, "If knowledge is power, Madison was a Titan."

A major *leitmotif* of Bennett's eminently readable history is America's conflicted treatment of the institution of slavery, culminating in the bloody Civil War and the Emancipation Proclamation. "The moment came," Lincoln explained, "when I felt that slavery must die that the nation might live." That the United States was willing to fight a protracted, murderous war on behalf of the freedom of a subjugated population cemented America's unique place in the world as a beacon of freedom for all people. America proceeded to bind up the wounds resulting from the fratricidal conflict and the institution of slavery (though many years passed before the civil rights of black Americans were fully recognized) before entering an industrial age that was "more golden than gilded." The first volume of *America* ends with a Serbian assassin's bullet precipitating a war "more total than anything previously seen" in history.

"We've got to teach history based not on what's in fashion but what's important," President Reagan concluded in his Farewell Address. Bennett does this in *America* because he understands, in the words of historian Walter Isaacson, that the role of the historian is "to inform, inspire, and sometimes provoke." Bennett's book is straight-up, old-fashioned American history.

The Age of Reagan: The Fall of the Old Liberal Order 1964–1980, Steven F. Hayward (2001)

The prominent liberal historian Alan Brinkley wrote in 1994 that 20th century American conservatism had been something of "an orphan in historical scholarship," in part because of "a basic lack of sympathy for the Right among most [liberal] scholars." Brinkley urged fellow historians to recognize and write about the significant role of the Right in 20th century America.

Several young conservative scholars have stepped forward and are writing highly praised works about American conservatism. A rapidly rising star of the conservative intellectual movement is Stephen Hayward, who, in *The Age of Reagan*, proposes to do for Ronald Reagan what the liberal historian Arthur Schlesinger, Jr., did for FDR: to make the man and his times one and the same. Hayward succeeds in his big, bold, and ambitious book, which covers the period from 1964 to the Reagan Presidency in 1980 and is the best historical biography yet written about Ronald Reagan.

Hayward argues that Reagan became President because of his extraordinary political skill, often underrated persistence, and unwavering conservative philosophy and because of the rapid decline of liberalism in the 1960s and 1970s. In smashing the monopoly of liberalism in 1980, Hayward says, Reagan "exposed the fractured and increasingly hollow character of what passes for liberalism in the late twentieth century" and prepared the way for the robust conservative side of the debate now prevailing in much of American politics. Hayward, a smooth and appealing writer, makes a strong case for his assertion that the closing decades of the past century can properly be called the "Age of Reagan."

Our Country: The Shaping of America from Roosevelt to Reagan, Michael Barone (1990)

There are certain books that people must have: The Christian needs the Bible, the constitutional lawyer needs *The Federalist Papers*, and the political junkie needs *Our Country*. *Our Country* is a dazzling political history of America from the 1930s to the 1980s by Michael Barone, the favorite political analyst of everyone from conservative columnist George Will to the late liberal Democratic Senator Daniel Patrick Moynihan.

Rejecting the progressive argument that American politics centers on economics—"who gets what, when, and how"—Barone argues rather that (1) our politics divide along cultural rather than economic lines; (2) in wartime, Americans tend to choose expanded government power and cultural uniformity while, in peacetime, they want smaller government and cultural diversity; and (3) individuals matter. Towering over everyone in 20th century America, in Barone's view, is Franklin D. Roosevelt, who shaped America through the Great Depression and World War II. Much of the shaping of the American political scene since FDR was done by Presidents Lyndon Johnson and Ronald Reagan, two admirers of FDR with far different political principles and goals.

Our Country is an enticing mix of shrewd electoral analysis and political trivia. Readers will discover how the civil rights movement gained political power, why Richard Nixon was the first presidential candidate to campaign in all 50 states, and why Reagan won overwhelmingly in 1980 (not because of Jimmy Carter's political ineptitude but because the voters liked Reagan's ideas of limited domestic policy and a more assertive foreign policy). Long admired for editing the authoritative *Almanac of American Politics*, Barone offers in *Our Country* a commanding narrative of a country whose fundamentals of political democracy and economic freedom are "the basis of any good society."

TOTALITARIANISM

*D*ominated by the Janus-like ideologies of Nazism and Communism, the 20th century was the cruelest century in human history. Several hundred million people died in the wars, concentration camps, famines, purges, and executions initiated by the two "isms."

In the category of TOTALITARIANISM, we suggest 11 books that describe the ideologies of Nazism and Communism; the attempts of dictators like Hitler, Stalin, and Mao to rule the world; and the West's sometimes uneven but ultimately victorious response to their plans of conquest.

Communism: A History, Richard Pipes (2001)

Communism, the sanguinary tyranny that controlled more than 30 nations and was responsible for the deaths of an estimated 100 million people during the 20th century, suddenly collapsed without a shot being fired. In just two years, from 1989 to 1991, the Berlin Wall fell, the Soviet Union dissolved, and Marxism–Leninism was dumped unceremoniously on the ash heap of history. Only a superlative historian calling on a lifetime of study could sum up the reasons for so precipitate a collapse in a single slim volume.

In *Communism: A History*, Harvard professor and renowned Sovietologist Richard Pipes states that "Communism was not a good idea that went wrong; it was a bad idea." Marxism, the theoretical foundation of Communism, carried within it the seeds of its own destruction because it argued that private property is a "transient...phenomenon." No less flawed was Marxism's notion that human nature is "infinitely malleable" and can be refashioned at will. Communist regimes were forced to resort to "merciless" violence (one of Lenin's favorite adjectives) and a dictatorship of the bureaucracy to maintain power. As soon as "reformers" like Gorbachev tampered with the system, it developed fissures and "flew apart." Communism was doomed to fail, Pipes says, because it was "a pseudo-science converted into a pseudo-religion and embodied in an inflexible political regime."

Although Pipes concentrates on the Soviet Union (the first one-party state in history), he also examines Communism's deleterious impact in the West and the Third World. One surreal example: Deprived of Soviet financial aid, Fidel Castro was forced to tout the advantages of Cuban prostitution, declaring that his country had the lowest incidence of AIDS in the world. The historical record is clear, Pipes concludes: All countries living under Communism experience a sharp decline in living standards and the emergence of a supreme leader—the antithesis of the Marxist vision of freedom for all. *Communism: A History* is a concise and compelling introduction to an informed understanding of the movement that marred so much of the 20th century.

The Rise and Fall of the Third Reich: A History of Nazi Germany, William L. Shirer (1960)

How did a fanatical leader and the political movement he headed bring about the first truly global war and engineer the most grisly genocide of the 20th century? Journalist William Shirer recounts the rapid rise and swift fall of Nazi Germany in this monumental study. Adolph Hitler and his henchmen boasted when they came to power in Germany in 1933 that the Third Reich would last 1,000 years, but their "evil empire" crashed and burned in the spring of 1945, vanquished by a mighty crusade for freedom led by Supreme Allied Commander Dwight D. Eisenhower. In *The Rise and Fall of the Third Reich*, Shirer combines "you are there" reporting—he personally covered Nazi Germany's rise to power for ABC News from Vienna and Berlin—with impressive scholarship. Among his Matterhorn of sources were 485 tons of records from the German Foreign Office and stenographic records of 51 "Fuehrer Conferences."

Although Shirer witnessed it all firsthand, he underestimated Hitler's maniacal designs at the time. "How can a country go into a major war with a population so dead against it?" he wrote in his diary in 1939. Writing after the end of World War II, Shirer admits that this was a "naïve question." Hitler had been preparing for war for years; he only needed the right moment to give the order, which came when Britain's Neville Chamberlain surrendered Czechoslovakia to Hitler in the infamous 1938 Munich Agreement.

Throughout his career, Hitler made no secret of his plans to rearm Germany, invade its neighbors, and kill Jews—more than 6 million by the end of World War II. These horrific actions are thoroughly documented in the 1,250 pages of *The Rise and Fall of the Third Reich*, which won the National Book Award and is still the best-selling title in the history of the Book of the Month Club. Shirer's work remains a forceful reminder of the power of evil and the necessity to resist it before it is too late.

The God That Failed, André Gide, Richard Wright, Ignazio Silone, Stephen Spender, Arthur Koestler, Louis Fischer (1950)

When six of the world's most famous writers explain why they became Communists and then rejected Communism, it is a confession heard 'round the world. The writers were black American novelist Richard Wright, Italian realist writer Ignazio Silone, French Nobel Prize–winner André Gide, Hungarian novelist Arthur Koestler, British editor Stephen Spender, and American foreign correspondent Louis Fischer. The one thing that linked these six very different men was that all of them chose Communism in the 1920s and 1930s because they had lost faith in Western democracy and values. Desiring an end to poverty and war, they turned to Communism only to discover that its promises were all lies. The words "brotherhood" and "freedom" were only slogans. Truth was whatever the Communist Party said it was. The very things for which the six Western intellectuals had joined the party were most endangered by the party itself.

In *The God That Failed*, Koestler writes, "At no time and in no country have more revolutionaries been killed and reduced to slavery than in Soviet Russia." Gide says, "I doubt whether in any country in the world...have the mind and the spirit ever been less free, more bent, more terrorized over and indeed vassalized than in the Soviet Union." Fischer declares, "Nineteen years after the fiery birth of the Bolshevik regime, ubiquitous fear, amply justified by terror, had killed revolt, silenced protest, and destroyed civil courage." The charges of the indictment are like relentless blows of a mighty hammer, tearing apart the facade of Communism and leaving its countless crimes and victims exposed for all to see. Louis Fischer reflects the anger and revulsion of his once-Communist colleagues when he says, "I see that I turned to Soviet Russia because I thought it had the solution to the problem of power.... I now realize that Bolshevism is not the way out because it is itself the world's biggest agglomeration of power over man."

Because of its utter honesty and eloquence, *The God That Failed* is an invaluable document about the "ism" that held nearly half the world captive at the height of the Cold War.

Witness, Whittaker Chambers (1952)

Whittaker Chambers was a veteran Soviet spy who became, in William F. Buckley Jr.'s words, "the most important American defector from Communism." Chambers tells the story of his youthful disillusion with the West, participation in espionage (with the likes of Alger Hiss) at the highest levels of our government, and final break with Communism in this best-selling autobiography. Among the many conservatives who have cited *Witness* as a book that changed their lives are President Ronald Reagan, former *National Review* publisher William A. Rusher, and columnist and commentator Robert Novak.

Published in 1952, *Witness* argues that America faces a transcendent, not transitory crisis; that the crisis is not one of politics or economics but one of faith; and that secular liberalism, the dominant "ism" of the day, is a watered-down version of Communist ideology. The New Deal, Chambers insists, is not liberal democratic but "revolutionary" in its nature and intentions.

The book is permeated with what Buckley called "Splenglerian gloom." In renouncing Communism, Chambers believes that he is probably leaving the winning side but finds reason to keep fighting against Communism for the sake of his children. In "A Foreword in the Form of a Letter to My Children," Chambers writes that Communism is "the central experience of the first half of the 20th century and may be its final experience" unless the free world discovers a "power of faith" that will provide two certainties: "a reason to live and a reason to die." In the face of the West's latest challenge—radical Islamism—Chambers's trenchant words are as relevant today as they were when first written half a century ago.

The Great Terror: Stalin's Purge of the Thirties, Robert Conquest (1968)

What atrocities have Communist dictators such as Joseph Stalin committed to deserve the label of "monster"? The distinguished historian Robert Conquest provides an authoritative answer about Stalin in *The Great Terror*, described by one reviewer as "an odyssey of madness, tragedy, and sadism." Conquest writes that the 1930s purge by which Stalin made himself the unchallenged ruler of the Soviet Union had three distinctive aspects: its immense scale, in which "millions perished and every member of the population was held under immediate threat"; the extraordinary device of the "confession trial," with the dictator's former colleagues and critics publicly denouncing themselves for treason; and its secrecy—nothing was officially said of the vast operation that extended from the Lubyanka prison in Moscow to the Gulag (forced labor camps) in Siberia.

For years, many Western intellectuals accepted the Soviet explanation that Stalin's actions were a necessary response to a vast "Trotskyite" conspiracy that had penetrated every aspect of Soviet life. Conquest exposes this lie in *The Great Terror*, first published in 1968 and based mainly on unofficial sources. He published a reassessment in 1991, using material obtained from the Soviet archives that, the author says, "shows things to be rather worse than I originally suggested." For example, about a million Communist Party members were killed on Stalin's order as well as 30,000 military officers, including 80 percent of the generals and colonels, all potential challengers to his rule. The total population of the Gulag was 12 million to 15 million, with 10 percent to 20 percent of the prisoners dying in the first year.

Although *The Great Terror* is generally accepted, even in Russia, as an accurate account of the period, historian Paul Johnson has pointed out that the crimes committed by Stalin and his henchmen "have never been atoned for, properly investigated or punished (except by accident)" because the Communist leaders who ruled after Stalin, from Khrushchev to Brezhnev, were all involved in them. As a result, Conquest says, Russia still lives under Stalin's shadow.

The Gulag Archipelago, Alexander Solzhenitsyn (1973)

This is an indispensable book for conservatives interested in the terrible truth about the vast network of forced labor camps that held millions of prisoners in the former Soviet Union. It is all here, wrote Russian author Lydia Chukovskaya: "search, arrest, interrogation, prison, deportation, transit camp, prison camp...hunger, beatings, labor, corpses." *The Gulag Archipelago* is far more than a blood-chilling history of the camps; it is an examination of the core ideology of Communism and the other "isms" of the 20th century. For Solzhenitsyn, the great Russian novelist and historian, who spent eight years imprisoned in the camps and 20 years in internal exile in the Soviet Union before being expelled to the West, "the principal trait of the *entire* twentieth century is that men have forgotten God." Against this atheism, says his biographer Edward Ericson, Solzhenitsyn counterposes "a moral vision rooted in Christian teaching."

Solzhenitsyn understood how important *The Gulag Archipelago* was: "Oh, yes," he said, "*Gulag* was destined to affect the course of history, I was sure of that." It delegitimized the

Soviet government among Russians and discredited it in the West. It was Solzhenitsyn who named the camps "Gulag," a word now used universally to denote forced labor camps or prisons created especially for political dissidents. As Ericson points out, *The Gulag Archipelago* deliberately shifts the focus from the high-ranking victims of Stalin's purges and terror to the ordinary Russians, Ukrainians, and other nationalities who "perished by the millions as a result of the insane effort to create a new man and a new society." For his many works, Solzhenitsyn was awarded the Nobel Prize for Literature in 1970.

The Gulag Archipelago is a profound work: part history, part memoir, part spiritual essay about the role of "redemptive suffering" and the need to oppose every form of tyranny over the mind and soul of man.

The Captive Mind, Czeslaw Milosz (1953)

Why did many Eastern European intellectuals in the post–World War II era so easily accept and even embrace totalitarian thinking? Because, writes the Polish poet and devout Catholic Czeslaw Milosz in *The Captive Mind*, religion had ceased to exist as a force, and Communism filled the void. Faithless intellectuals quickly converted to the New Faith because, feeling alienated from society, they had a great longing to belong to the masses: Communism satisfied that sociopolitical longing. These same intellectuals proved themselves capable of rationalizing anything, even the loss of their own intellectual freedom. Milosz calls this mental state *ketman*, a way of holding two contradictory ideas simultaneously that is akin to George Orwell's "doublethink."

Milosz profiles four members of the Polish intelligentsia that he personally knew, recounting their gradual ceding of creative independence to the government. A former Catholic novelist is reduced to making speeches against the Vatican. A poet who survived Auschwitz becomes an anti-American hack journalist and commits suicide. A poor country boy becomes a trusted Communist Party member, ambassador to a Western European country, and then "the political overseer of all the writers" in Poland. A gifted but alcoholic poet returns from exile to Poland, where the party finds him so unreliable that he is reduced to translating the comedies of Shakespeare—a humiliating assignment that he willingly accepts.

The Captive Mind, for which Milosz won the Nobel Prize for Literature in 1981, is a rich, multi-layered examination of how totalitarian regimes, both Communist and fascist, control the intellectual life of a nation. At the center of that control is "the crushing weight of an armed state." If the center should ever lose its material might, Milosz writes prophetically, "it is not hard to imagine" that "millions of obedient followers of the New Faith" would "suddenly turn against it." By reason of its insights into the totalitarian mind and its political pre-science, *The Captive Mind* deserves an honored place alongside Orwell's *1984*.

Suicide of the West: An Essay on the Meaning and Destiny of Liberalism, James Burnham (1964)

In the year that President Lyndon B. Johnson trounced conservative challenger Barry Goldwater at the election polls and liberalism seemed destined to dominate American politics for the foreseeable future, James Burnham, a former Trotskyist turned conservative thinker, published an audacious book depicting liberalism as "the ideology of Western suicide." The West, he argues in *Suicide of the West*, has been in territorial retreat and civilizational decline since World War I, having apparently lost its will to survive. Among the reasons he gives are "the decay of religion," "an excess of material luxury," and the pernicious influence of modern liberalism.

Drawing on his formidable analytical skills, Burnham lists 19 beliefs of liberalism such as the ideas that human nature enjoys "an indefinite potential for progressive development" and government has a duty to guarantee everyone "food, shelter, clothing and education, and security against unemployment, illness and the problems of old age." Liberal government, Burnham says, poses an especially serious danger at this time because of three crucial challenges: the threat of Soviet Communism, the political mobilization within the Third World, and the skyrocketing crime rate. Liberalism, "infected" with Communism, falsely assumes that the true enemy is always on the Right.

James Burnham gained fame, as historian Richard Pipes writes, with the publication in 1941 of *The Managerial Revolution*, in which he stated that in the modern world, entrepreneurial capitalists were being replaced by professional administrators—a thesis that influenced George Orwell in writing *1984*. Burnham's description of the basic flaws of modern liberalism in *Suicide of the West* holds true to the present day.

To Build a Castle: My Life as a Dissenter, Vladimir Bukovsky (1978)

"Since ancient times man has been accustomed to regard three things as the most terrifying on Earth: death, madness, and imprisonment." Soviet dissident Vladimir Bukovsky, the author of these words, confronted and survived all three in the post-Stalin Soviet Union through his indomitable will and genius for survival. *To Build a Castle* is his memoir, the story of a young Russian rebel expelled from school at 17 for starting an unauthorized magazine, sent to a psychiatric hospital at 22 for leading poetry readings in the center of Moscow, and imprisoned at 24 for publicly defending Alexander Ginzburg and other dissidents. Bukovsky spent 12 years in Soviet prisons, labor camps, and *psikhushkas*—forced-treatment psychiatric hospitals filled with political prisoners. He was expelled from Soviet Russia in 1976, not long after Alexander Solzhenitsyn.

The "castle" in the book's title refers to the structure Bukovsky drew on scraps of paper, on the floor and walls of isolation cells, and in his mind: "a castle in every detail, from the foundations, floors, walls, staircases, and secret passages right up the pointed roofs and turrets." It was a place where he entertained guests, drank wine, read books, and barred his captors. The castle, he writes, "saved my life."

To Build a Castle is a mesmerizing book that tells of stubborn prisoners who hold hunger strikes, sympathetic women orderlies who slip apples or cheap candy to the emaciated "patients" in the psychiatric hospitals, and Bukovsky's secret meetings with Western journalists between arrests. The journalists precipitated an international uproar with their stories about the widespread Soviet abuse of psychiatric institutions. *To Build a Castle* is the inspiring story of one man's "impossible" victory over a seemingly omniscient state.

Political Pilgrims: Travels of Western Intellectuals to the Soviet Union, China, and Cuba 1928–1978, Paul Hollander (1981)

Why have so many noted Western intellectuals—from George Bernard Shaw to Jean-Paul Sartre to Susan Sontag—waxed so enthusiastic over the decades about Communism, even at its most repressive? Paul Hollander explores this intriguing question in *Political Pilgrims*, a seminal study of Western visitors to Soviet Russia, Communist China, Castro's Cuba, and other "socialist" states whose observations often border on the pathological. An English Quaker wrote that "the Communist view of human nature seems to me far more inspired by Faith, Hope, and Charity than our own." Dismissing the existence of the Gulag, a criminologist asserted that in the Soviet Union, "the whole idea of punishment has been frankly dropped and the aim of reformation alone pursued." About the infamous trumped-up Moscow trials of the 1930s, *The New York Times*'s Walter Duranty wrote, "It is unthinkable that Stalin…and the Court Martial could have sentenced their friends to death unless the proofs of guilt were overwhelming." British socialists Beatrice and Sidney Webb insisted that Stalin was not a dictator or a despot but "a duly elected representative" of the Supreme Soviet of the USSR.

Cuba remains an unfailing favorite of those on the American Left who feel an urgent need for an alternative to their own country, which they find dull, conformist, and lacking in idealism and "social conscience." The hero worship of dictator Fidel Castro expressed by Sontag, Saul Landau, Abbie Hoffman, and many others is hilarious and depressing at the same time. Of China, where an estimated 50 million people have died in socialist experiments such as the Great Leap Forward and the Cultural Revolution, John K. Fairbank, America's leading Sinologist, wrote, "The Maoist revolution is on the whole the best thing that happened to the Chinese people in centuries."

Unlike one-time leftists Gide, Koestler, and Silone, who rejected Communism and publicly explained why (see *The God That Failed*, page 76), few of the intellectuals examined in *Political Pilgrims* have recanted. They acknowledge no accountability for their earlier follies; they avoid any possibility of being tarred with the brush of anti-Communism. They are caught, Hollander explains, in an intricate web of utopianism, secularization, and alienation, all of which breeds an abiding contempt for the West. What most concerns Hollander, however, is not the intellectuals' praise of a particular Communist state but the cumulative impact of their denigration of Western society. *Political Pilgrims* is a powerful book, much quoted and imitated over the years, recently by Mona Charen in her best-selling study about the enemies of Western civilization, *Useful Idiots*.

The Black Book of Communism: Crimes, Terror, Repression, Stéphane Courtois *et al.* (1999)

An estimated 6 million European Jews died in the Nazi Holocaust during World War II. This monstrous act of genocide—the deliberate annihilation of an entire people—confirmed Nazism's uniquely evil nature. But with the opening of official archives in the former Soviet bloc and other sources, Communism has been revealed as guilty of terror, torture, famine, mass deportations, and massacres on an unprecedented international scale.

According to *The Black Book of Communism*, Communism killed 85 million to 100 million people over a period of seven decades. The toll included 6 million deaths from famine in Ukraine in the early 1930s, 7 million banished to the Soviet Gulag before World War II, at least 30 million Chinese dead during the so-called Great Leap Forward, and an estimated 1.7 million deaths in the killing fields of Cambodia—one-sixth of the country's entire population. Stéphane Courtois and the other French authors of *The Black Book of Communism* do not simply provide statistics. They tell, for example, of the helpless children of Cambodia who were hung from the roof by their feet and kicked until they died. As to why the Communists practiced wholesale murder, Courtois, a former member of the French Left, points to their "purely abstract vision of death, massacre and human catastrophe," rooted in Lenin's willingness to achieve ends by any means necessary.

The Black Book of Communism, a best-seller in France and in much of the rest of Europe, is a careful accounting of the violent crimes of Communism that proves, as Courtois puts it, that Stalin, Mao, and Pol Pot were far better at killing than at governing.

WORLD HISTORY

*"M*any people know less history than their parents or grandparents had known," historian John Lukacs has written, "but more people are interested in history than probably ever before." The popularity of works by David McCullough, Joseph Ellis, Richard Brookhiser, and others about the American Revolution and the Founders attests to the strong public interest in American history. Lukacs's statement also applies to Americans' abiding curiosity about world history. As a nation of immigrants, we have always been drawn to the history of our forebears, cognizant that to understand ourselves we must understand the world from which we came.

In the category of WORLD HISTORY, we offer books by seven eminent historians, including Paul Johnson on the birth of the modern world and Jacques Barzun on the past 500 years of the cultural life of the West.

Europe: A History, Norman Davies (1996)

Because the majority of Americans have European roots, speak a European language (English), and are shaped by European culture, they should have some understanding of the history of Europe in order to better understand themselves. An excellent place to start is Norman Davies' one-volume *Europe: A History.* At more than 1,000 pages, it is not a short work, but

Davies is a vigorous writer with a keen eye for major political, cultural, and economic trends, from the rise of Christianity to the collapse of Soviet Communism, as well as the curiosities and sideshows that overly serious historians often overlook. Ukraine, for example, is the land through which "the greatest number of European peoples approached their eventual homeland." There are 300 such arresting "capsules" scattered throughout the book.

Europe takes the reader from an unnamed peninsula (the term "Europe" was not widely adopted until the late 18th century) through ancient Greece and Rome, the "Middle Age," and the Enlightenment to a landmark of European history: the French Revolution. "There is a universal quality about the French Revolution," Davies writes, "which does not pertain to any of Europe's many other convulsions." A penultimate chapter describes the Europe of the 19th century when it was "the powerhouse of the world." The book ends with the Europe of the 20th century, initially divided by two wars and two "isms" (Nazism and Communism) and then united with the collapse of Communism and the emergence of the European Union.

Europe is grand panoramic history that constantly engages the reader, largely because Davies, instead of feeling compelled to *explain* Europe, is content to describe it.

Dynamics of World History, Christopher Dawson (2002)

In our overwhelmingly secular world, it is a brave historian who writes, "God not only rules history: He intervenes as an actor in history." Likewise, in our quantitative world—dominated by numbers and statistics—it is a rare writer who asserts, "The essence of history is not to be found in facts but in tradition." And in our ever-rational world, it is a man of unusual conviction who serenely refers to the "irreducible element of mystery" in history. All of these statements were made by Christopher Dawson, a major historian of the mid-20th century who had a significant influence on such conservative giants as Russell Kirk and T. S. Eliot.

Acclaimed by the liberal *Saturday Review of Literature* in 1950 as an "unequalled" historian of culture, Dawson fell out of favor with the establishment because of his insistence that religion is at the center of every culture. But as Western civilization lost contact with the spiritual sources of its creative power while achieving its greatest material triumph, the critic John J. Mulloy says, scholars began to revisit the work of Christopher Dawson, the quintessential Christian writer and independent English scholar who ended up at Harvard University.

Dynamics of World History offers 26 essays in which Dawson examines how ancient and modern civilizations have decayed because of "spiritual disillusionment"; the triumph of the bourgeoisie over Bolshevism in England and elsewhere; and the Christian view of history ("St. Augustine sees history as the meeting point of time and eternity"). He deftly profiles Marx, Spengler, and Toynbee and argues that, despite its secularism and self-centeredness, Western culture is still marked by a moral and spiritual dynamism inherited from its Christian past that will outlast "political ideologies and economic empires."

The Roads to Modernity: The British, French, and American Enlightenments, Gertrude Himmelfarb (2004)

Liberals have long insisted that the French Enlightenment, and only the French Enlightenment, with its emphasis on reason rather than religion and its exaltation of ideas such as universal rights and progress, inaugurated the modern world. But what if there were other enlightenments as important to a proper understanding of modernity?

In *The Roads to Modernity*, Gertrude Himmelfarb, one of our most distinguished intellectual historians, describes three enlightenments: the French, representing the ideology of reason; the British, with its sociology of virtue; and the American, with its politics of liberty. All three had common traits, such as respect for reason and liberty, science and industry, justice and welfare, but they also had profoundly different political consequences. It was not the radical French Enlightenment but the moderate British Enlightenment, with thinkers such as Adam Smith and Edmund Burke, that created a moral and social philosophy that was humane and realistic—a philosophy that profoundly shaped the American Enlightenment and resonates to this day in our society.

Himmelfarb explains how America, more than any other country, has retained Adam Smith's vision of political economy, a "system of natural liberty" that governs the polity as well as the economy. What other nations regard as an inexplicable paradox Americans take for granted, says Himmelfarb: The United States is at once the most capitalistic and the most moralistic of countries.

From Dawn to Decadence: 500 Years of Western Cultural Life, 1500 to the Present, Jacques Barzun (2000)

Only the polymathic Jacques Barzun could have written, at the age of 93, *From Dawn to Decadence*, a one-volume cultural history of the past 500 years. In a sweeping and entertaining manner, the book explores pivotal events, critical trends, and unexpected personalities. We meet Martin Luther, Leonardo da Vinci, and François Rabelais, but also Marguerite of Navarre and Christina of Sweden, as the author seeks to unfold the intricate plot woven by the actions of men and women "whose desires are the motive power of history." The history is divided into four periods: 1500–1660, dominated by religion and matters of faith; 1661–1879, concerning what to do about the status of the individual and the mode of government; 1790–1920, concerning how to achieve social and economic equality; and 1921 to the present, representing the mixed consequences of all these trends.

Born in France but educated in the United States and then associated with Columbia University for almost 50 years, Barzun shows that from 1500 to the present, the West offered the world "a set of ideas and institutions not found earlier or elsewhere," producing a unique blend of unity and diversity. As the West carried these ideas to the extreme, however, the result was decline and decadence. Thus, we have the deadlocks of our time: movements for and against nationalism, for and against individualism, for and against the high arts, for and against strict morals and religious belief.

Barzun notes as a sign of uncertainty the proliferation of descriptive labels about our period: the age of the masses, the age of globalism, the age of communication, the age of anger, the age of anxiety, etc. Nevertheless, he is no apostle of angst. Decadence is the normal end of great periods of history, he says: a necessary prelude to the creative impulse that will inevitably erupt, especially among the young and talented "who keep exclaiming what a joy it is to be alive."

Civilization on Trial, Arnold J. Toynbee (1948)

Acknowledging that history is the story of the rise and fall of civilizations, noted British historian Arnold Toynbee determined to answer the question, "Why do civilizations die?" In his classic A Study of History, Toynbee identifies 23 civilizations and concludes that breakdown and disintegration were caused not by things such as the environment, race, or political and military expansion, but by three factors: a failure of creative power in the ruling minority, a withdrawal of allegiance by the majority, and the loss of social unity in society at large. In his epic work, Toynbee presents a relativistic, even patronizing view of religion as supplementary to civilization.

To the shock of his secular admirers, Toynbee reverses himself in *Civilization on Trial*, declaring, "Civilizations are the handmaidens of religion." He states that the "higher religions," especially Christianity, have brought about "an immeasurable improvement in the conditions of human social life on Earth." He rejects the "dreary" cyclic theory of history first promulgated by Greek intellects such as Aristotle and later adopted by Hegel. The coming "world-embracing civilization," he suggests, will be essentially religious.

Civilization on Trial offers a wide-ranging vision of our past and possible future. It also contains a special bonus: a succinct 47-page summary of Toynbee's *A Study of History* by Oxford historian D. C. Somervell.

The Birth of the Modern: World Society 1815–1830, Paul Johnson (1991)

If we were asked when the modern world was born, most of us would probably point to the 1780s—the decade of the French Revolution, the American Constitution, and Britain's emerging industrial economy. But in *The Birth of the Modern*, the eminent British historian Paul Johnson argues that while modernity was conceived in that turbulent decade, its actual birth was delayed until after the Napoleonic Wars and the War of 1812 when, in an era of peace and a balance of powers, unprecedented political, economic, and demographic changes could have their full effect.

From 1815 to 1830, for example, the United States transformed itself from a struggling ex-colony into "a formidable nation." Russia began to develop the "fatal fissures" that engulfed her in the 20th century. Latin America came into an "independent and troubled" existence. The age, Johnson points out, abounded in great politicians like Andrew Jackson, the first President elected by an overwhelming popular vote; radical philosophers like Georg Wilhelm Friedrich Hegel; and revolutionary musicians like Ludwig van Beethoven. There appeared life-changing inventions like the railway and the steam printer, which enabled the daily press to set the pace of political change in advanced societies, inspiring one observer to dub the press "the Fourth Estate."

Like all of Johnson's histories, *The Birth of the Modern* is big (over 1,000 pages) and exciting; the reader is swept along on a torrent of vivid language as the author describes the many factors responsible for the world's advance toward "the democratic age." They include the growth of literacy, the rapid rise in population and incomes, the spread of technology and industry, the diffusion of competing ideas, and the actions of great men and women. Johnson subscribes fully to the dictum that history is made by men (and women), and he proves once again in *The Birth of the Modern* that histories can be inspiring as well as educational.

The Second World War, Volume I: The Gathering Storm, Winston S. Churchill (1948)

How fortunate that a great statesman and wartime leader endowed with a surpassing literary talent has given us his personal account of the global conflict that still affects the politics of our world. *The Gathering Storm* is a riveting history of the accelerating series of events—the mistakes of the Allies after World War I, the rise of Mussolini and Hitler, the tragic outcome of Munich—that led to the outbreak of World War II. It is also a fast-paced autobiography in which Churchill warns of the growing threat of Nazi Germany and prepares himself to lead Great Britain against that enemy.

Political analysis at the highest level, the book's major lesson is that a powerful enemy like Nazism will not be turned away by appeasement and accommodation but must be met with force and resolution. Writing at the beginning of the Cold War, Churchill was warning the West about the danger of appeasing the Soviet Union and Communism. His warning is equally relevant today in the war against terrorism.

A master of words—whether in Parliamentary debate, a rallying speech to a beleaguered nation, or written history—Churchill describes his confident state of mind in May 1940 as he forms a government: "I felt as if I were walking with Destiny, and that all my past life had been but a preparation for this hour and this trial.... I was sure I should not fail." *The Gathering Storm* is splendid history, written by the man who made it, and justifies the judgment of the editors of *Human Events*, who described it as the number one book on leadership in time of war.

WORLD POLITICS

*B*efore globalism, it was generally accepted that all politics is local. Today, with the existence of "24/7" stock markets, mass media, and weapons of mass destruction, one hears more frequently that all politics is global. What happens in Baghdad, Mexico City, London, or Beijing matters not only to policymakers in Washington, D.C., but also to ordinary Americans in Charlotte, Columbus, and Seattle.

In the category of WORLD POLITICS, we offer six books on such topics as the critical role of statecraft (Margaret Thatcher), what went wrong in the Middle East (Bernard Lewis), and a new history of the Cold War and its aftereffects (John Lewis Gaddis).

The Cold War: A New History, John Lewis Gaddis (2005)

The Cold War was America's longest conflict, lasting more than four decades and taking a heavy toll in life and treasure: All told, more than 90,000 American servicemen lost their lives in the Korean and Vietnam Wars. The Cold War was a global war, pitting America and the free world against the Soviet Union and its satellites on every continent, sometimes in battle, sometimes in negotiation. Harrowing incidents like the Cuban Missile Crisis, the brutal Soviet crushing of the Hungarian Revolution, and the Soviet invasion of Afghanistan intensified the tension between the two superpowers. More than 15 years after the end of the Cold War, we are still grappling with what happened and why it happened. For example, how large a role did Joseph Stalin play in the instigation of the Korean War? How close to nuclear war did we come in the Cuban Missile Crisis? Answers to these and other questions are essential to a proper understanding of the defining struggle of the latter half of the 20th century.

In *The Cold War: A New History*, John Lewis Gaddis, the dean of Cold War historians, provides a crisp and comprehensive survey of this epic conflict. He gets most of the essential points right. The Soviet Union, and not the United States, was primarily responsible for the Cold War. Communism promised a better life but failed miserably—one need only look at the perennial breadlines in Soviet Russia and the disastrous Great Leap Forward of Mao Zedong in China. President Reagan, along with Margaret Thatcher and John Paul II, ultimately led the West to a peaceful victory after years of near-war. "Reagan was as skillful a politician as the nation had seen for many years," Gaddis writes, "and one of its sharpest grand strategists ever."

The Cold War has some minor flaws. Gaddis is overly laudatory about Mikhail Gorbachev's role in ending the war—which was passive rather than proactive—and assigns too much credit to diplomat George Kennan, arguing that his "long telegram" of 1946 formed the basis of U.S. strategy toward the Soviet Union throughout the Cold War. Nevertheless, Gaddis has provided us with an authoritative account of the war and of the heroes, on both sides of the Iron Curtain, who first challenged and then defeated Communism.

Dictatorships and Double Standards: Rationalism and Reason in Politics, Jeane J. Kirkpatrick (1982)

The salience of one magazine article has never been better demonstrated than in the appearance of "Dictatorships and Double Standards" in the November 1979 issue of *Commentary*. The article was written by Jeane Kirkpatrick, a respected but relatively unknown professor of government at Georgetown University and a life-long Democrat, who had written speeches for the proto-liberal Hubert Humphrey and supported Senator Henry "Scoop" Jackson for the 1976 presidential nomination. By the late 1970s, however, Kirkpatrick had become disenchanted with the feckless foreign policy of President Jimmy Carter. She chose the pages of the neoconservative journal *Commentary* to state bluntly, "The failure of the Carter administration's foreign policy is now clear to everyone except its architects."

Under Carter, she points out, there occurred a dramatic Soviet military buildup, matched by the stagnation of American armed forces, and a dramatic extension of Soviet influence in the Horn of Africa, Afghanistan, southern Africa, and the Caribbean, matched by a declining U.S. position in the same areas. Kirkpatrick is especially critical of the Carter Administration's proactive role in Iran and Nicaragua, where anti-Communist autocrats friendly to America had been replaced with unfriendly autocrats of an "extremist persuasion." Carter and his advisers applied a double standard, she writes, accepting the status quo in Communist nations but not in nations ruled by so-called right-wing dictators. In so doing, Kirkpatrick charges, the Carter Administration "violated the strategic and economic interests of the United States."

Presidential candidate Ronald Reagan read Kirkpatrick's article and liked it so much that he invited her to become a member of his foreign policy advisory team. Upon his election, Reagan appointed her U.S. Ambassador to the United Nations, where she forcefully defended American interests. President Reagan's unquestioned success in the area of foreign policy was due in no small measure to the exemplary performance of Jeane Kirkpatrick and other neoconservatives such as Richard Perle, Max Kampelman, and Elliott Abrams. *Dictatorships and Double Standards* includes the penetrating *Commentary* article as well as other essays on U.S. foreign relations, totalitarian thought, party reform, and the Constitution that reflect Kirkpatrick's special ability to expose the fallacies of foreign policy utopianism and moralism as well as liberals' lack of realism in policymaking.

Statecraft: Strategies for a Changing World,
Margaret Thatcher (2002)

Soviet Communism toppled and the Cold War ended without a major military confrontation primarily through the statesmanship of U.S. President Ronald Reagan, British Prime Minister Margaret Thatcher, and Polish Pope John Paul II, as confirmed in Thatcher's impressive treatise *Statecraft*. Like its author, the first woman to serve as Britain's prime minister, the book is both principled and pragmatic. Despite the enormous impact of "globalism" on our lives, argues Thatcher, nation-states retain a fundamental importance because they alone set legal frameworks, provide a sense of identity, and retain "a monopoly of legitimate coercive power." At the same time, the pursuit of statecraft without regard for the moral principles that undergird every democratic state "is all but impossible."

Observing the world in light of the terrorist attacks of September 11, 2001, Lady Thatcher reminds us that we have learned yet again that we live in a world of risk, conflict, and latent violence that requires enduring vigilance. The most reliable guardian of freedom in the world, she says, is America, not merely because of its military might or its economic strength but because of its entrenched values of freedom and civil society. Referencing Tocqueville, Thatcher points out that Americans hold religion "to be indispensable to the maintenance of republican institutions." America's faith, Lady Thatcher says, including its faith in itself and its mission of freedom, "is the bedrock of its sense of duty" to the nation and the world.

Statecraft reflects the virtues of a political leader whose partnership with President Reagan was the driving force of a conservative revolution that transformed the political landscape of the West and changed history.

Of Paradise and Power: America and Europe in the New World Order, Robert Kagan (2003)

"Americans are from Mars and Europeans are from Venus." With this provocative observation, respected foreign policy scholar Robert Kagan begins his analysis of the conflicted U.S.–European relationship and examines whether the breach can be repaired. He argues that for Europeans, the end of the Cold War eliminated not only a frontline adversary, the Soviet Union, but also "the need for geopolitics" of the *realpolitik* kind. There was now no problem, Europeans concluded, that could not be solved by diplomacy and international law.

But American Administrations from 1991 on continued their strategic and force planning, propelled by the requirements of the Persian Gulf War, conflicts in Bosnia and Kosovo, and the war on terrorism. Kagan points out the resulting paradox: The European "paradise"—idealistic and ever harmonious—is dependent upon America's willingness to use its military might "to deter or defeat those around the world" that still practice power politics. Nevertheless, says Kagan, Europeans, especially in "old" Europe, regard the prospect of "an American Leviathan unbound" as more threatening than the risks from terrorism and tyrants.

Of Paradise and Power was a national best-seller, widely praised for its impressive command of history, elegant writing, and brevity (it is only 158 pages long). Neoconservatives have often cited *Of Paradise and Power* for its assertion that in order to be true to its nature, America must promote liberal democracy, "not only as a means to greater security, but as an end in itself."

What Went Wrong? Western Impact and Middle Eastern Response, Bernard Lewis (2002)

For a thousand years, the world of Islam considered itself the leader in human civilization and achievement. Beyond its borders were only "barbarians" and "infidels." Islam represented the greatest military power on Earth, its armies invading at the same time Europe, Africa, India, and China. It was the foremost economic power with a far-flung network of commerce and communications. At the peak of its power in the mid-16th century, it had achieved the highest level yet known in the arts and sciences. Medieval Europe was "dependent of the Islamic world," relying on Arabic translations of classical Greek texts. Yet by the early 18th century, Islam not only had been soundly defeated on the battlefield and on the high seas, but also was being superseded in the marketplace by the same barbarians it had scorned. Today, compared with its millennial rival, Christendom, the world of Islam is generally judged to be "poor, weak, and ignorant." What went wrong?

Bernard Lewis, one of the West's foremost experts on Islamic history and culture, begins by explaining that the Renaissance, the Reformation, and the technological revolution "passed virtually unnoticed in the lands of Islam." There is also the sacrosanct subordinate status of the woman and the unbeliever (*dhimmitude*). And the ideal Islamic state, he points out, is a theocracy, putting Islamic law at the center of politics and society.

In attempting to determine the reasons for Islam's decline and fall, Lewis says, many in the Middle East have blamed others, the villains ranging from the Mongols to the Turks to the Americans. Fundamentalists point to the adoption of alien practices and the falling away from "authentic Islam." Modernists cite the scarcity of secular democracies such as the Turkish Republic as the reason for the comparative lack of development. To the Western observer, Lewis writes, the reason is clear: The lack of freedom in every area, from politics to economics to culture, is the major source of stagnation. To become a great center of civilization, he concludes in his fascinating book, the peoples of the Middle East must abandon grievances, settle differences, and join their talents and resources in "a common endeavor."

The Clash of Civilizations and the Remaking of World Order, Samuel P. Huntington (1996)

With the dissolution of the Soviet Union in December 1991 and the end of the 45-year Cold War, two paradigms about the future of global politics emerged. One school of thought, led by political scientist Francis Fukuyama, predicted "the universalization of Western liberal democracy" and a world that would be generally harmonious. The other school, represented by Harvard professor Samuel P. Huntington, was not so sanguine, arguing that competing cultures and cultural identities would dominate a multipolar world. "Clashes of civilizations," Huntington wrote, "are the greatest threat to world peace." Huntington's prediction has seemingly been substantiated by the political developments and military conflicts of the post–Cold War world.

In *The Clash of Civilizations*, Huntington makes a fourfold argument, asserting that the world is "multi-civilizational"; that the balance of power is shifting from the West to the East; that the West's universalist dream is bringing it into conflict with other civilizations, especially Muslims; and that the "survival of the West depends on Americans reaffirming their Western identity." While Huntington acknowledges the importance of China's remarkable economic progress—it took the United States 47 years to double its per capita output; China did it in ten—he devotes major attention to what he calls the "Islamic Resurgence."

Islamic states and societies, he says, are reinstituting Islamic law in place of Western law, increasing the use of religious language and education, adhering more closely to Islamic codes of social behavior, and expanding their efforts to develop international solidarity. However, the movement from Islamic consciousness to Islamic cohesion is hampered by the absence, so far, of an "Islamic core state."

Huntington's advice, in light of declining Western power, is for America and the European countries to achieve greater political, economic, and military integration; encourage the "Westernization" of Latin America; slow the drift of Japan away from the West; and recognize that Western intervention in other civilizations is "the single most dangerous source of instability and potential global conflict" in a "multi-civilizational" world.

PUBLIC POLICY

$\mathcal{T}$he political crises facing America often seem never-ending—out-of-control government spending and regulations, an ever-expanding welfare state, waves of illegal immigrants, an escalating war on terrorism. But Americans are nothing if not problem-solvers, and modern conservative leaders have excelled at providing practical solutions to "intractable" problems. We can put America back on course, says President Ed Feulner of The Heritage Foundation, by insisting that "our government behaves in accordance with American traditions and values. We cannot allow a nation conceived in true liberty under higher law to tolerate limitless government power."

In the category of PUBLIC POLICY, we offer six books that exemplify conservative thinking about how to move the nation in the right direction in the areas of welfare, crime, and foreign policy.

Losing Ground: American Social Policy 1950–1980,
Charles Murray (1984)

That a single book can bring about a fundamental change in public policy is proven by *Losing Ground*, in which Charles Murray documents and exposes the dysfunctional American welfare system. Murray shows that the percentage of Americans in poverty had been dropping since World War II, but those trends slowed in the late 1960s and then stopped in the mid-1970s, precisely when government spending on poverty programs rose sharply. Welfare programs that were supposed to lift people out of poverty did just the opposite: They undermined the American work ethic, fostered a culture of dependence, and created a permanent underclass.

Murray proposes specific welfare reforms such as limiting assistance to those who are genuinely unable to work, attaching a stigma to anyone who is able-bodied and on welfare, and rewarding those who "achieve" more than those who do not. Conceding that an "entrenched social service bureaucracy" would fiercely resist these changes, Murray insists that such changes are necessary to construct a true safety net that will raise "the poor to independence."

It took a while, but Murray's controversial findings have become the new orthodoxy. In 1996, after twice vetoing the welfare reform proposed by a Republican Congress, President Bill Clinton signed into law a workfare program that made welfare support temporary rather than permanent and no longer an entitlement. *Losing Ground*, commented *The New York Times*, was the "book that many believe begat welfare reform." Since then, the national welfare rolls have declined by half, the child poverty rate has fallen to its lowest level in history, and welfare as we once knew it is no more. None of this would have been possible without *Losing Ground*, one of the most consequential public policy books of the past quarter-century.

The Dream and the Nightmare: The Sixties' Legacy to the Underclass, Myron Magnet (1993)

Of all the titles in *Reading the Right Books*, probably none got under the skin of modern liberals more than Myron Magnet's *The Dream and the Nightmare*. Building on the research of Charles Murray's *Losing Ground*, which judged the Great Society to be a trillion-dollar failure, Magnet declares that it was the 1960s counterculture—not Ronald Reagan, as many liberals contend—that divided the nation into haves and have-nots and created today's underclass.

The sexual revolution, he argues, transformed American values and behavior, thereby increasing divorce, illegitimacy, and the number of families headed by single mothers. The "personal liberation" philosophy of the haves undermined the attitudes that traditionally moved people up the economic ladder: qualities such as deferral of gratification, sobriety, thrift, and dogged industry. In effect, Magnet writes, the new culture held the poor back from advancement "by robbing them of responsibility" and "squelching their initiative and energy." However well-meaning their intentions, the haves imposed what most Americans knew to be wrong: the parceling out of rewards on the basis of race and the freeing of violent criminals on technicalities.

Magnet's solution: Stop the current welfare system; stop quota-based affirmative action; stop treating criminals like justified rebels; stop letting wrongdoers live in public housing at public expense; and stop "Afrocentric education" in the schools. One politician who was impressed by Magnet's analysis was George W. Bush, who said that *The Dream and the Nightmare* "crystallized for me the impact [that] the failed culture of the '60s had on our values and society."

Thinking About Crime, James Q. Wilson (1975)

Long before New York City Mayor Rudy Giuliani adopted a strategy of "broken windows"—policing that focuses on eliminating so-called petty crime—and criminologists concluded that repeat offenders were Public Enemy Number One, political scientist James Q. Wilson wrote *Thinking About Crime*. Relying on his close study of law enforcement and crime, Wilson boldly challenges a number of widely held beliefs. Inner-city residents, he finds, do not despise the police or refuse their aid. It is not true that crime can be dealt with only by attacking its "root causes." That is like saying that "stupidity can only be dealt with by attacking its root causes." The public understands far better than many criminologists, Wilson says, that the principal causes of crime are to be found in the attitudes formed by family and peer group. Massive federalization of crime enforcement is not the answer.

Rather than arguing that we can eliminate crime by eliminating poverty, as the Left does, or by simply putting more police on the street, as some on the Right do, Wilson proposes a series of prudential steps calculated to achieve "modest success." He focuses on the problem of "habitual offenders," too many of whom suffer "little or no loss of freedom." He cites one study showing that the rate of serious crime would be one-third as great as it is now if every person convicted of a serious offense were imprisoned for three years. The federal government, Wilson says, should resist spending more and more billions on crime control programs that *ought* to work and concentrate on those that actually *do* work. Crime prevention, he reminds the reader, is essentially a state and local governmental responsibility.

It is important, Wilson says, to think about crime as a part of human nature as well as about the criminal acts themselves. Wilson argues that a proper understanding of man and the forces to which he will respond, coupled with moderate expectations, is "the essential place to begin any discussion of crime and its control."

To Empower People: From State to Civil Society, Peter L. Berger and Richard John Neuhaus (1996)

Pamphlets have always played a prominent role in our political history: Thomas Paine's *Common Sense* was read by one out of every six colonists; William Lloyd Garrison and other abolitionists widely distributed their anti-slavery tracts; Barry Goldwater's landmark book *The Conscience of a Conservative* (see page 17) is essentially an extended pamphlet. In 1976, on the 200th anniversary of the Declaration of Independence, there appeared a 45-page pamphlet, *To Empower People*, which introduced a new term in the political lexicon: "mediating structures." The appeal of mediating structures—defined as the institutions standing "between the individual in his private life and the large institutions of public life"—reverberated across the ideological spectrum. In the wake of the Great Society and other failed liberal experiments, both the Left and the Right were ready to consider a new answer to Aristotle's fundamental question about how we ought to order our life together.

Like all effective political pamphlets, *To Empower People* is succinct, readable, and timely. It is based on an idea that goes back at least as far as Edmund Burke's defense of the "little platoons" of society against the calculated abstractions of the French Revolution. Berger and Neuhaus focus on four structures—neighborhood, family, church, and voluntary association—arguing that they are "essential for a vital democratic society." They list the characteristics of American society that favor the enhancement of mediating structures, including our immigrant nature, our relative affluence, our stability, our sense of tolerance and fair play, and our relatively strong civic institutions.

In an expanded 1996 edition, which includes an introduction by neoconservative commentator Michael Novak and several commentaries on the original work, Berger and

Neuhaus reassert the purpose of *To Empower People*: to inspire everyday citizens to rediscover "the excitement of the American experiment" based on the ability of the American people "to govern themselves in freedom."

Statecraft as Soulcraft: What Government Does, George F. Will (1983)

Since the founding of the Republic, Americans have debated an essential question: How much government do we need? Two hundred years ago, it was the national government Hamiltonians versus the "states' rights" Jeffersonians. During the first half of the 20th century, it was FDR and the Progressives versus Taft and the old guard Republicans. Within the conservative movement, this debate has continued in more recent times between traditionalists such as Russell Kirk and classical liberals or libertarians such as F. A. Hayek.

In *Statecraft as Soulcraft*, celebrated conservative commentator and columnist George Will calls for a politics based on civility, piety, and cooperation—a tradition that began in Athens and has been repeatedly enriched through the centuries by such leaders as Cicero, Burke, Tocqueville, and Lincoln. Modern America, Will argues, has acquired political values that involve a "disproportionate individualism" and an "inadequate sense of human beings as social creatures." He urges a "strong government conservatism" based not on self-interest or utopian notions but on a "great given—natural right."

Will explains that he is not proposing the subordination of the individual to society, but rather "a healthy accommodation" between the individual and society. Echoing Robert Nisbet and Irving Kristol, he says that government must have and encourage a sense of community rooted in shared values and aims. The role of statecraft as soulcraft, he concludes, is not to promote a particular view of Social

Security, public works, or nuclear deterrence but to help achieve "the optimum equilibrium of liberty and equality." Small wonder that Russell Kirk, an apostle of ordered liberty, praised Will's polished book as "an exhortation demanding political views imaginative and humane."

The Tragedy of American Compassion, Marvin Olasky (1992)

A fundamental error of those who are in charge of government welfare programs—at least until the 1990s—was the belief that money could eradicate poverty and solve the social problems of America's underprivileged. But the more government expended on Aid to Families with Dependent Children (AFDC) and similar programs, the greater the number of people who wound up below the poverty line and on welfare. Liberal policymakers were distraught. If money was not the answer, and if the programs of the welfare state did not work, what was left? A Texas professor provided a startling answer: Study how Americans helped Americans for more than two centuries before the coming of the welfare state and replicate their efforts in the modern era.

In *The Tragedy of American Compassion*, Marvin Olasky shows how Americans for many decades generously fulfilled their Judeo–Christian responsibility to help those in need in their communities. One example among hundreds is the Salvation Army, which in 1900 had 20,000 volunteers and was finding employment for 4,800 persons per month. The Army and similar groups observed "seven seals of good philanthropic practice," including stressing the importance of family ties, bonding between helper and helped, focusing on long-term employment, and the critical relationship between spiritual and physical needs. "Many lives can be saved," writes Olasky, who did his initial research as a Bradley Fellow at The Heritage Foundation, "if we recapture the vision that changed lives…when our concept of compassion was not so corrupt." The corruption, says Olasky, was implanted by the New Deal and institutionalized by the Great Society, which transformed the traditional American idea of a helping hand into a government entitlement.

Then-House Speaker Newt Gingrich elevated *The Tragedy of American Compassion* to best-seller status with an enthusiastic recommendation. The historic welfare reform of the 1990s owes much to Olasky's pioneering research, as does the faith-based initiative of President George W. Bush.

POLITICAL
CULTURE

*T*here has been agreement since the founding of the Republic that a good society requires good men and women. As John Adams put it, "Public virtue is the only foundation of republics." George Washington argued that the inalienable rights that Americans enjoyed required a commitment to moral duty and civic virtue. More recently, political philosopher Michael Novak wrote that "as human lungs need air, so does liberty need virtue."

In the category of POLITICAL CULTURE, we offer five books that explore the interaction between politics and culture in modern America in such areas as the destructive counterculture of the 1960s and the controversial Supreme Court decisions that banned prayer in public schools and discovered a constitutional right to an abortion.

The Closing of the American Mind, Allan Bloom (1987)

When Allan Bloom, a Professor of Classics at the University of Chicago, published his withering criticism of relativism and multiculturalism on the American campus along with a stout defense of the great books and thinkers of Western Civilization, he was condemned as racist, sexist, and elitist by the high priests of political correctness. Liberals were incensed by Bloom's attacks on such cultural phenomena as rock music, which he said "encourages passions and provides models that have no relation to any life" that young people can possibly lead. Most conservatives agreed that Bloom gave a powerful account of the central problem in American higher education, but some said that his solution fell short: They wanted faith as well as reason to be acknowledged as central to society. *The Closing of the American Mind* became one of the most talked-about books of the decade and a best-seller with a million copies in circulation.

The American academy, Bloom writes, has abandoned the liberal arts (that is, classical liberal learning) and has adopted either the latest intellectual fads or retreated to their academic specialties. As a result, a profound "crisis" confronts the American academy. Bloom's Platonic solution is simple (some conservatives would say simplistic): Provide "a good program of liberal education" and feed "the student's love of truth and passion to live a good life." Educational historian Christopher J. Lucas said that Bloom was extending an argument made earlier by E. D. Hirsch, Jr., of the University of Virginia, who believed that America was dangerously close to losing "its coherence as a culture" and that "we need to connect more of our students to our history, our culture, and those ideas which hold us together."

The Closing of the American Mind deserves to be read by each new generation of conservatives, editor Adam Bellow argues, because it launched a conservative counterattack against political correctness and the liberal monopoly in universities. It is requisite reading for anyone who, in the words of Thomas Pangle, wants to map "the moral continent we sleepily inhabit." Bloom's work is that rare book that makes you think—deeply and seriously.

The Tempting of America: The Political Seduction of the Law, Robert H. Bork (1990)

Advocates of constitutional originalism despaired when Federal Judge Robert Bork was denied a seat on the Supreme Court, but there was a silver lining in the Senate's reprehensible action: It inspired the constitutional scholar and leading proponent of "original understanding" to write *The Tempting of America*, a powerful weapon in the conservative campaign for judges who interpret the Constitution as written.

The need to place prudential judges on the bench is self-evident. The most disturbing trend in modern American law has been the transformation of the Supreme Court from impartial judicial arbiter into intrusive policymaker. Driven by socioeconomic rather than judicial considerations, the Court has interpreted the Constitution so as to ban prayer in public schools, establish a constitutional right to abortion, permit Congress to regulate the nation's non-economic activity, and allow the guilty to go unpunished because of incidental, technical errors in evidence gathering.

The Tempting of America shows that from the earliest years of our Republic, there has been a desire to use the Court to attain political ends. Bork traces how the Constitution came to be viewed not as settled law but as judicial clay to be molded at political whim. An activist judge, Bork says, "can reach any result." He states flatly that our tripartite system of government was not designed to handle arbitrary laws handed down by nine unelected judges without accountability to the other two branches of government. The book provides an added benefit: Judge Bork's review of his nomination battle and the absurdities of the charges leveled against him: Senator Ted

Kennedy, for example, charged that confirmation of the distinguished jurist would lead to an America where "women would be forced into back-alley abortions, blacks would sit at segregated lunch counters...the doors of the federal courts would be shut on the fingers of millions of citizens." All of which demonstrated how far liberal politicians were willing to go to keep a conservative like Robert Bork off the Supreme Court.

For those who seek a deeper understanding of the originalist view of the Constitution by a distinguished jurist and forceful writer, *The Tempting of America* is a must.

Liberal Parents, Radical Children, Midge Decter (1975)

Long satisfied to call herself a liberal anti-Communist, a disillusioned Midge Decter broke with the American Left in the 1960s because it rejected the idea that America was "a just and good society," even equating it with Nazi Germany. She joined other former liberals such as Irving Kristol, Norman Podhoretz, Jeane Kirkpatrick, and Michael Novak in a movement that became known as neoconservatism. (*Reading the Right Books* lists works by all of them.) An "action intellectual," Decter founded the Committee for the Free World, a group of pro-Western writers and thinkers who saw the Soviet system as a clear threat to America's basic freedoms.

An equally important contribution was her sharp critique of the culture war engulfing the nation and the role played by the "destructive generation" of the sixties. In *Liberal Parents, Radical Children*, Decter argues that the parents of her generation (often referred to as the "greatest generation") failed to discharge their fundamental responsibility of passing on to their children the importance of character, standards, and the notion of right and wrong. As a result, their wayward children eagerly embraced the counterculture with its contempt for authority, taste for drugs, and sense of entitlement. But civilization, Decter argues, depends on the cultivation of moral discipline among children, "the long slow slogging effort that is the only route to genuine maturity of mind and feeling."

Heritage President Ed Feulner notes that Midge Decter is always commonsensical and practical, linking her insights to "the concrete realities of life—motherhood, marriage, striving, and hoping." She argues without illusions and without fear: a truly free and liberated woman.

Who Stole Feminism? How Women Have Betrayed Women, Christina Hoff Sommers (1994)

"I am grateful. . .to the students of my women's studies *ovular* at Washington University." So remarked feminist philosophy professor Joyce Treblicot, for whom the term "seminar" was "offensively masculinist" and had to be replaced with a more "woman-friendly" term. This and other examples of radical feminism are highlighted in Christina Hoff Sommers' trenchant critique of the contemporary women's movement. Sommers refers to the "new wave" of feminism since the 1960s as "gender feminism." Gender feminists see every aspect of women's lives as dictated by an "oppressive" and "patriarchal" system. The only solution, they assert, is an overhauling of society and politics. These gender feminists contrast sharply with the "equity feminists" of an earlier generation— women such as Susan B. Anthony and Elizabeth Cady Stanton, who fought for the *equal* participation of men and women in education and the workplace.

Sommers argues that the gender feminists have done far more damage than good for women because they constantly encourage conflict between the sexes and a victim mentality among women. Surveys suggest, however, that an increasing number of American women reject the militant agenda of the gender feminists and their methodologically questionable research.

Gender feminism, nevertheless, is pervasive on America's campuses, where "Women's Studies" departments have grown from a small subject area to a prominent fixture in the curriculum. These departments are known for their radical politics, intolerance of criticism, lack of intellectual rigor, and hostility toward men. They are quick to label anyone who disagrees with them as "insensitive," "misogynistic," or "sexist." Such practices have helped to foster political correctness and dumbed-down curricula, adversely affecting the education of both men and women.

Who Stole Feminism? is a convincing indictment of the ideologues who hijacked the feminist movement, deliberately distorting the data and manipulating politicians along the way.

The Clash of Orthodoxies: Law, Religion, and Morality in Crisis, Robert P. George (2001)

Just as intellectual historian Russell Kirk refuted the liberal cliché of the 1950s that conservatism was a movement without a mind, so has public philosopher Robert George effectively disproved the liberal argument of the 2000s that the conservative position on social issues such as abortion and same-sex marriage is "mere religion," bereft of rationality. In *The Clash of Orthodoxies*, George demonstrates that traditional Judeo–Christian principles employ faith *and* reason—"the two wings on which the human spirit rises in contemplation of truth," in the words of the late John Paul II. Judeo–Christian principles were, in fact, the foundation of America's regime of freedom and equality as set forth in the Declaration of Independence and the Constitution: a truth, the author points out, that is too often ignored by the Supreme Court.

Using natural law philosophy, George exposes the fallacies of orthodox secularism, such as its argument that the very young and the very old are "subpersonal instruments" and therefore not entitled to full legal protection. He also challenges secularism's call for so strict a separation of church and state that there should be no legislation based on "the religiously informed moral convictions of legislators or voters."

Written for the general reader and not the political philosopher, *The Clash of Orthodoxies* addresses front-page issues such as embryonic stem cell research and abortion and what the appropriate policy response of orthodox Christians and Jews should be. In a chapter on religious values and politics, George, himself a Catholic, calls upon his co-religionists to return to what he calls "old-fashioned liberalism," honoring limited government, the rule of law, and private property as well as social justice and the common good.

UNCONVENTIONAL THOUGHT

*S*tarting with William F. Buckley Jr. over 50 years ago, modern conservatives have frequently been required to be unconventional and even radical in their thinking and writing, confronted as they have been by the liberal zeitgeist. Even the prototypical traditional conservative Russell Kirk described himself as "a bohemian Tory."

In the category of UNCONVENTIONAL THOUGHT, we offer works by six of the most unconventional individuals in America: Bill Buckley, P. J. O'Rourke, Norman Podhoretz, David Horowitz, Dinesh D'Souza, and Shelby Steele. Prepare yourself for a walk on the wild side of conservatism.

Miles Gone By: A Literary Autobiography, William F. Buckley Jr. (2004)

It has been estimated that between 1951, when he wrote his first book, and 2000, William F. Buckley Jr. wrote 35 non-fiction books; 15 novels; 56 introductions, prefaces, and forewords to other people's books; 227 obituary essays (a Buckley specialty); more than 800 editorials, articles, and commentaries in *National Review* (which he founded in 1955); more than

350 articles in other periodicals; and over 4,000 syndicated newspaper columns. He also hosted *Firing Line*, the longest-running public affairs program in TV history, gave guest lectures at the rate of 70 appearances a year, sailed across the Atlantic and Pacific oceans on his yacht, and ran for mayor of New York City. Once asked why he kept so busy, Buckley drawled, "I am easily bored."

In *Miles Gone By*, Buckley offers a selection of previously published writings that limn "a narrative survey of my life, at work and play." The personally chosen pieces reveal what matters most to a (even *the*) founder of the modern American conservative movement. They are, in order, his family, his friends, and his travels. Buckley writes movingly about the two colleagues who had the greatest political influence on him— Whittaker Chambers (see page 77) and James Burnham (see page 81)—and reveals on nearly every page his determination to live every day to the fullest.

There is plenty of conservative politics in *Miles Gone By*, and there are piquant stories about *National Review*, which he counts as his most significant achievement. He is especially proud of one subscriber, Ronald Reagan, whom he describes as "the principal political figure of the second half of the 20th century." Buckley has said he will never write a formal autobiography but hopes that *Miles Gone By* will serve "much the same purpose and that it will give pleasure." Indeed it does.

Parliament of Whores: A Lone Humorist Attempts to Explain the Entire U.S. Government, P. J. O'Rourke (1991)

The federal government has long been the irresistible target of America's humorists, from Mark Twain to Will Rogers to one of today's best political satirists, P. J. O'Rourke. He begins *Parliament of Whores* with these arresting words: "What *is* this oozing behemoth, this fibrous tumor, this monster of power and expense hatched from the simple human desire for civic order?" For the next 232 pages, O'Rourke offers a hilarious lesson in civics, stating that it is not true that the government "wastes vast amounts of money through inefficiency and sloth." Rather, he insists, "enormous effort and elaborate planning are required to waste this much money."

O'Rourke is an equal opportunity satirist, lampooning the moral posturing of both political parties and the utopian plans of bureaucrats. There is no poverty in America, he declares; citing Heritage senior analyst Robert Rector, he says that in 1963 a "poor" American family had an income 29 times greater than the average per capita income in the rest of the world. He writes that after two years of studying the political machinations in Washington, D.C., he has learned the great lesson that "giving money and power to government is like giving whiskey and car keys to teenage boys." O'Rourke finishes his book not with a quip but with a painful political truth: "Every government is a parliament of whores," and in a democracy, "the whores are *us*."

Along with Ben Stein, Christopher Buckley, Rush Limbaugh, and others, O'Rourke has demolished the canard that conservatives are dull and predictable. His biting wit is on full display in *Parliament of Whores*.

Making It, Norman Podhoretz (1967)

If Irving Kristol is the godfather of neoconservatism, Norman Podhoretz is the prodigal son. Precocious as a child growing up in Brooklyn, and brilliant as a student at Columbia University and Cambridge University, 23-year-old Podhoretz burst onto the New York literary scene in 1953 with a withering review of Saul Bellow's *The Adventures of Augie March*, which almost everyone else had praised as a great American novel. Podhoretz was subsequently invited to write for *Partisan Review* and *The New Yorker*, the leading liberal magazines of the day. He later joined the editorial staff of *Commentary*, becoming editor-in-chief of the prominent monthly in 1960. At the ripe young age of 30, he had "made it."

Like Kristol, however, Podhoretz kept bumping into reality. Never a Stalinist or an America-hater, he became increasingly critical of "the Family," the New York intellectual elite of which he had once yearned to be a part. He rejected their rabid anti-anti-Communism and their love affair with the radical New Left. As he writes in *Making It*, he refused to echo the charges that America was intrinsically "racist or imperialistic or counterrevolutionary." His editorial impulses became more political and less literary, transforming him from the golden boy of the New York Left to a prominent spokesman of the American Right.

Making It is authentic Podhoretz: provocative, insightful, and personal. It is the arresting memoir of the son of immigrant Jews who became one of the most influential intellectuals in America. The British historian Paul Johnson compares Podhoretz to George Orwell, but Norman Podhoretz is really that rarest of all creatures—an original.

Radical Son: A Generational Odyssey, David Horowitz (1997)

While it is not surprising that a young Jewish intellectual with Communist parents would become a leader of the radical Left in America, it is startling when that same intellectual publicly rejects Marxism and becomes a prominent conservative. In *Radical Son*, David Horowitz describes his deep involvement with the Left: as an anti-war activist at Berkeley; as an editor of the radical 1960s magazine *Ramparts*, which revealed, in violation of the Espionage Act, that the National Security Agency had cracked the Soviet intelligence code; and as a confidant of

Black Panther leader Huey Newton. But Horowitz experienced an "internal free-fall" when a *Ramparts* coworker was murdered by the Panthers, who were suddenly revealed to be not civil rights champions but criminal thugs.

Following a period of deep personal and philosophical examination, Horowitz joined the Right in the early 1980s, endorsing President Reagan and the Contras in Nicaragua. He explains his remarkable ideological metamorphosis: "It was what I thought was the humanity of the Marxist *idea* that made me what I was then; it is the inhumanity of what I have seen to be the Marxist *reality* that has made me what I am now."

What he is now is one of the most quoted conservatives in America. Through the David Horowitz Freedom Center, his writing, and his frequent lectures, he closely monitors liberal excesses, especially on the modern college campus. Horowitz, perhaps more than anyone else on the Right, is able to enrage the radical Left; after all, he used to be one of them. *Radical Son* is vintage Horowitz: forceful, intellectually honest, and moving.

Illiberal Education: The Politics of Race and Sex on Campus, Dinesh D'Souza (1991)

Political correctness might have prevailed on America's campuses were it not for revealing works like Dinesh D'Souza's *Illiberal Education* and the author's vigorous promotion of the book on television and radio and in dozens of collegiate debates. D'Souza reports that American universities, abetted by left-leaning faculty, deliberately filled a "sizable portion of their freshman class[es]" with minority students with little regard for their qualifications; diluted or displaced their core curricula to make room for new courses dealing with non-Western cultures, Afro-American studies, and women's studies; and set up and funded separate institutions for minority groups in the name of "pluralism" and "diversity." The alarming result was a basic transformation of American higher education—and not for the better.

After surveying conditions at the University of California at Berkeley, Stanford, Howard, the University of Michigan, Duke, and Harvard, D'Souza concludes that affirmative action has increased rather than decreased racial and gender tensions. Born in India and himself a person of color, D'Souza warns that if the university model is replicated in society at large, it will "reproduce and magnify the lurid bigotry, intolerance, and balkanization of campus life in the broader culture."

Books like *Illiberal Education*, a model of careful research and rhetorical clarity, and Allan Bloom's *The Closing of the American Mind* (see page 111) inspired a powerful conservative reaction in the early 1990s against the divisive politics of race and sex on college campuses and in support of John Henry Newman's idea that the University should develop the attributes of "freedom, equitableness, calmness, moderation, and wisdom."

White Guilt: How Blacks and Whites Together Destroyed the Promise of the Civil Rights Era, Shelby Steele (2006)

What happened to Martin Luther King's shining dream of an integrated, color-blind America? Cultural critic and award-winning author Shelby Steele describes how the civil rights movement of the 1960s boldly challenged racial discrimination, insisting that America must honor democratic principles in practice as well as in theory, especially the idea that one's race must not lessen one's rights as an individual. The white liberal establishment admitted to the historical guilt of racism and discrimination and, in doing so, lost much of its moral authority. In a desperate attempt to recover legitimacy, writes Steele, liberal whites embraced government "handouts," affirmative action, ideologically motivated black studies departments at universities, and other programs to demonstrate their commitment to diversity and opposition to racism. In so doing, Steele argues, they further exploited blacks by viewing them as victims, not as equals. Tragically, in order to retain their authority, many black leaders have actively promoted the culture of victimization.

One of Steele's most perceptive insights is that white guilt has produced a new "liberalism of dissociation." Cleansed of racism, sexism, and militarism, the "dissociated man" is a new kind of American—supposedly a better kind of American because he has dissociated himself from the litany of American sins. In 2004, John Kerry ran as the "new man" presidential candidate against the unreconstructed George Bush and lost, proving, as Steele suggests, that the larger public, unlike some of the nation's institutions and the liberal elite, feels less and less need for dissociation.

Steele is not without hope. In the last chapter of *White Guilt*, he says that most of today's conservatives sound like the Martin Luther King of 1963, treating race with the same compassionate classical liberalism that King articulated in his "I have a dream" speech. He praises President Bush for offering a new direction for social reform in America: "dissociation from the racist past through principle and individual responsibility rather than at the expense of those things."

LITERATURE

We know from experience that a novel, play, or poem can have a significant and lasting influence on the reader. A famous example is the 1903 evangelical novel *That Printer of Udell's,* by Harold Bell Wright, which Ronald Reagan read at the age of 12. Reagan told his mother that he wanted to be like the novel's hero, who experiences a Horatio Alger ascent to personal and spiritual fulfillment. The novel ends with the hero setting out for Washington, D.C., to serve in the U.S. Congress.

For the LITERATURE category, we have selected 10 powerful novels by some of the best-known and best-selling authors of the 20th century.

1984, George Orwell (1948)

"Newspeak," "thought police," "Big Brother Is Watching You." Few works of fiction have contributed more enduring phrases to American culture and politics than George Orwell's novel *1984,* written, the author says, with a purpose to "alter other people's idea of the kind of society they should strive after." Warning against a ubiquitous, omnipotent government that molds the past and therefore the present, *1984* is a passionate defense of individual freedom.

Protagonist Winston Smith leads a dreary life within the even drearier city of London. As a clerk in the Ministry of Truth, he erases and corrects news items that question the infallibility of the government. The totalitarian system under which he lives regulates every aspect of existence, from food consumption to language, outlawing even the basic instinct of love. Smith joins what he thinks is an underground resistance movement set on undermining "Big Brother," but it turns out to be a trap set by the state. After extensive brainwashing, during which Smith is made to believe that two plus two equals five, he accepts that one comes to love oneself only by loving Big Brother.

Stalin's reign of terror and the Nazi Holocaust, as well as Mao Zedong's *laogai* and the Khmer Rouge's horrors in Cambodia, have transformed *1984* from a warning into a commentary on the modern era. Orwell's reputation as novelist and political prophet, more than that of almost any other writer of his generation, has risen steadily because of *1984*, one of the most influential novels of the 20th century.

Atlas Shrugged, Ayn Rand (1957)

Those who have not read Ayn Rand's classic novel *Atlas Shrugged* will have difficulty answering the question, "Who is John Galt?" But millions are familiar with the ultra-libertarian ideas espoused in her book, one of the most popular works of the 20th century. Rand called her philosophy "objectivism," while others have referred to it as "unfettered capitalism."

Atlas Shrugged is the epic story of the mysterious engineer and superman Galt, who rejects altruism and embodies a heroic egoism. His followers literally worship the dollar (Rand scorned Christianity and any notion of charity) and proclaim, "Greed is good." They vow to stop the world, already breaking down as a result of progressive taxes, government regulations, and other onerous government policies, and then build a new and wealthier world based purely on self-interest. While traditional conservatives are wary of Rand's unrestrained embrace of radical individualism and her disdain for religion, her biting criticism of the welfare state and planned economies is seconded by almost everyone on the Right.

At over 1,000 pages, *Atlas Shrugged* is long and didactic, but it is a perennial best-seller, especially among young people attracted by Rand's passionate paean to the individual. Libertarians invariably name *Atlas Shrugged* as their favorite novel and applaud its message: If everyone were allowed to act in his own best interest, we would all be better off.

One Day in the Life of Ivan Denisovich,
Alexander Solzhenitsyn (1962)

This Nobel Prize–winning novella, which first exposed the ugly, brutal reality of the vast network of Soviet concentration camps, begins: "The hammer banged reveille on the rail outside camp HQ at 5 o'clock as always." It ends in much the same fashion: "Shukhov felt pleased with life as he went to sleep. A lot of good things had happened that day. He hadn't been thrown in the hole.... He'd swiped the extra gruel at dinnertime.... He hadn't been caught with the blade at the search point.... Just one of the 3,653 days of his sentence, from bell to bell. The extra three days were for leap years."

On this one day, as Katherine Shonk points out in her perceptive introduction to the authorized 2005 edition, we share Ivan Denisovich Shukhov's cold, hunger, fear, and exhaustion as well as the brief comforts of a cigarette or a crust of bread that he snatches when the guards aren't looking. We are caught up in the language of the novel—a mix of peasant slang, prison jargon, and unsentimental reportage. We marvel at Shukhov's shrewd resourcefulness, his stubborn dignity (he will not beg for a cigarette butt), and his will to survive at temperatures of 40 degrees below zero in a Siberian camp. His endurance, we come to realize, is sustained by a belief in God and a willingness to pray.

Soviet leader Nikita Khrushchev personally approved the publication of *One Day in the Life of Ivan Denisovich* as part of his anti-Stalin campaign, but Soviet authorities soon reversed that decision and denied further publication of Solzhenitsyn's works. But it was too late: The truth had been told about the millions who lived and worked and died in the "Gulag Archipelago" (see page 79), setting in motion the forces that ultimately led to the collapse of Communism and the dissolution of the Soviet Union.

Death Comes for the Archbishop, Willa Cather (1927)

Only a gifted writer could capture the unbounded beauty of the American Southwest, where American, Mexican, and Indian cultures intersect and often collide. In *Death Comes for the Archbishop,* prize-winning novelist Willa Cather tells the story of a young French Catholic priest, Jean Latour, who comes to the untamed New Mexico territory in the mid-1800s as its first apostolic vicar.

For more than 40 years, Bishop Latour travels thousands of miles on horseback and mule, endures desert heat and mountain blizzard, disciplines rebellious Spanish priests, and befriends legendary figures like the famed trader and guide Kit Carson. He grows to respect deeply the stoic Navajo and Hopi Indians and ultimately builds a magnificent cathedral in Santa Fe. When he dies, Mexicans and Americans alike kneel in prayer and honor the old bishop for his enduring faith in the face of almost perpetual adversity.

Cather, best known for her stories of the Nebraska prairies, makes the southwestern desert and sky characters in their own right. "Elsewhere the sky is the roof of the world," she writes, "but here the earth was the floor of the sky." *Death Comes for the Archbishop* is an elegy to a mythic land and a requiem for a devout missionary who epitomizes the classic virtues of courage, justice, and wisdom.

Darkness at Noon, Arthur Koestler (1941)

While many Western intellectuals were condoning and even approving the infamous Moscow show trials of the 1930s, former Communist Arthur Koestler wrote *Darkness at Noon*, a masterful psychological novel that shows how a veteran Bolshevik comes to confess publicly to crimes he did not commit. As George Orwell wrote in his perceptive review of the book, such irrational confessions suggest the following explanations: (1) the accused were guilty; (2) the accused were tortured and perhaps blackmailed by threats to relatives and friends; or (3) the accused were driven by despair, mental breakdown, and party loyalty. The answer for Koestler is number three.

Rubashov, the novel's protagonist and a hero of the revolution, has been a Communist for so long that ideas such as justice and the truth have become meaningless. When the party demands that he confess to preposterous crimes, he at first refuses but then, weakened by lack of sleep and endless interrogation, agrees. Although disillusioned by the betrayal of the revolution by the dictator named No. 1 (obviously a portrayal of Joseph Stalin), Rubashov cannot bring himself to abandon the party to which he has committed his life. The "darkness" Koestler depicts so brilliantly in his novel flows inevitably from the murderous paranoia of a tyrant like Stalin and the absolute power of an ideology like Marxism–Leninism.

Midcentury, John Dos Passos (1961)

Literary giants walked the Earth in the 1920s and the 1930s. Novelists such as Ernest Hemingway, F. Scott Fitzgerald, and John Dos Passos wrote about expatriate Americans in the cafés of Paris and the mountains of Spain. They invented a new language that was deceptively simple and often cinematic to tell their stories. They were heralded as the chroniclers of a Lost Generation wandering in the uncomfortable peace between two world wars.

When Dos Passos published his anti-capitalist, pro-socialist *U.S.A.* trilogy, the Left hailed him as a writer of rare power and insight. But his romance with Communism faded, aided by the Stalinist purges of the 1930s and the bloody extremism of the Communists in the Spanish Civil War. He began to write novels about the struggle of the individual against "giant bureaucratic machines" and a series of histories about the American experiment with its intrinsic faith in freedom. The Left's enthusiasm about John Dos Passos waned and then disappeared.

In contrast to *U.S.A.*'s anti–free-market theme, *Midcentury* is an unflinching exposé of the widespread graft and corruption in the American labor movement. It is also a far-ranging commentary on American politics and society in general. Luminaries such as Samuel Goldwyn, Eleanor Roosevelt, Robert LaFollette, Jr., Douglas MacArthur, and Jimmy Hoffa are deftly depicted. Each impressionistic sketch, each headline clipped from a newspaper, each chapter about the fictional characters like labor organizer Terry Bryant and the old Wobbly Blackie Bowman illustrates the central theme of *Midcentury*: The disintegration of the West is inevitable whenever Western man denies himself nothing by obeying Freud and denies himself everything by following Marx.

Sword of Honour: The Final Version of the Novels, Men at Arms, Officers and Gentlemen, The End of the Battle, Evelyn Waugh (1962)

Every war produces its literary legacy, including great novels such as Tolstoy's *War and Peace*, Stephen Crane's *The Red Badge of Courage*, Hemingway's *A Farewell to Arms*, and Joseph Heller's *Catch-22*. Worthy of inclusion on this short list is *Sword of Honour*, a trilogy about World War II written by the British master of satire Evelyn Waugh. Best known for his comic novels of the 1920s and 1930s—*Scoop* may be the funniest book ever written about journalism—Waugh revealed a deeper side, first in *Brideshead Revisited* and then in this multi-layered story of the war in which he personally served with bravery and distinction.

The protagonist of *Sword of Honour* is Guy Crouchback, an "uncharacteristic" Englishman and devout Roman Catholic who wants to fight for his country. After a series of adventures in Glasgow, London, North Africa, and Crete, Guy winds up as the liaison officer with the "partisans" (that is, Communists) fighting the Germans in Yugoslavia. His companions along the way include the old Africa hand Apthorpe, with his precious portable commode, and others who should be enshrined in the pantheon of seriocomic characters. Waugh describes the many sides of war: the endless training, the all-too-short weekend leaves, the nervous anticipation on the eve of attack, the indiscriminate destruction of bombs, and the finality of a bullet through the heart. He shows how little separates the actions of the hero and of the coward. He tells of the affecting love affair between Guy and his former wife, Angela, whom he remarries although she is with child by another man. A fascinating subplot of the novel for historically astute conservatives is the successful efforts of a Kim Philby–like traitor within the British government to persuade Winston Churchill to support the Communist Tito rather than the nationalist Mihailovich in Yugoslavia.

Within the never-flagging pages of *Sword of Honour*, Evelyn Waugh captures almost perfectly the nobility, the horror, and the tedium—the blood, sweat, and tears—of man's most terrible pursuit: war.

Advise and Consent: A Novel of Washington Politics, Allen Drury (1959)

There had been no major political novel about Washington for decades when Allen Drury's *Advise and Consent* burst onto the scene and immediately became a best-seller, staying at the top of the lists for nearly two years. It received a Pulitzer Prize and was then transformed, first, into a Broadway play and then into a Hollywood movie directed by the award-winning Otto Preminger and featuring such stars as Charles Laughton, who played the wily Southern Senator Seabright "Seab" Cooley. Drury, who for many years covered the U.S. Senate for *The New York Times*, vividly portrays the political and personal conflicts of a President's desperate campaign to win Senate approval of his nominee for Secretary of State, Robert Leffingwell.

Drury deliberately flouts liberal assumptions: Leffingwell is a smooth, handsome opportunist who covers up his early flirtations with the Communist Party. The leader of the pro-Leffingwell forces in the Senate is an unprincipled "progressive" who publicizes a youthful sexual affair of Brigham Anderson, the chairman of the Senate Foreign Relations Committee, in order to undermine his reputation and opposition to the nominee. The President engages in political manipulations that would make Machiavelli blush. In the dramatic denouement, the Senate decisively rejects Leffingwell after a despondent Anderson commits suicide.

Although *Advise and Consent* is not a great novel on the level of Orwell's *1984* or Waugh's *Sword of Honour*, it is nevertheless an exciting one. Cooley, Anderson, Orrin Knox, and the other characters live and breathe and bleed, illuminating, in Drury's words, "the human strengths and weaknesses of democratic governance."

Invisible Man, Ralph Ellison (1952)

Ralph Ellison's *Invisible Man* is one of the most widely read and taught works of African–American fiction. It is the story of a naïve young Negro man and his humiliating and brutal experiences in the Deep South and on the streets of New York, which ultimately lead him to hole up in an abandoned Harlem basement, disillusioned but still determined to find his real identity. *Invisible Man* is a blunt and passionate reflection on the reality of American intolerance and cultural blindness.

But *Invisible Man* is not a politically correct novel of racial protest; it is a conservative novel, imbued with a deep respect for individual freedom and responsibility and a clear rejection of both Black Nationalism and Communism. Ellison has stated his belief that democratic government and writers share similar goals: A democracy seeks to develop "conscious, articulate citizens," while novelists try to create "conscious, articulate characters." Ellison considered *Invisible Man* to be "a study in comparative humanity, which…any worthwhile novel should be." From a sharecropper's shack to a Communist rally, the anonymous young protagonist of *Invisible Man* wrestles with the gap that exists between the principles of America's democracy and the practices of its citizenry. In the epilogue, he concludes: "Life is to be lived, not controlled; and humanity is won by continuing to play in the face of certain defeat. Our fate is to become one, and yet many."

Employing the many voices of America—black and white, upper-crust and low-brow, religious and secular—*Invisible Man* challenges readers to act upon the ideals they profess to love so dearly.

The Bonfire of the Vanities, Tom Wolfe (1987)

During the 1980s, when President Ronald Reagan was changing the course of American politics, New Journalist Tom Wolfe wrote a novel that reinvigorated American fiction. Most novels at the time were thin autobiographical slices of life, usually written from a politically correct point of view. Nowhere to be seen was the big novel that dealt with the big issues of the day from a conservative perspective.

Wolfe's *The Bonfire of the Vanities* stunned American readers with its spellbinding, realistic tale of a New York City populated by greed-driven Wall Street denizens (dubbed "Masters of the Universe"); corrupt politicians; self-serving and exploitative black leaders (including the appropriately named Reverend Bacon); tabloid newspaper hacks; and a few heroes. It is, as critic Terry Teachout put it, an old-fashioned book written in "a newfangled style," the brash exclamatory voice of Wolfe's 1960s journalism. The novel soared to number one on the *New York Times* best-seller list and stayed there for months.

The huge success of *The Bonfire of the Vanities* signaled a comeback for the naturalistic novel in America. *Bonfire* is riveting reading, prompting one reviewer to say that it is as though the Coen and Marx brothers together had dramatized *The Great Gatsby*.

ABOUT THE
AUTHOR

LEE EDWARDS is Distinguished Fellow in Conservative Thought in the B. Kenneth Simon Center for American Studies at The Heritage Foundation.

A prolific writer, Dr. Edwards has been published in *National Review*, *The American Spectator*, *Policy Review*, and *Reader's Digest* as well as such leading newspapers as the *Wall Street Journal*, *Los Angeles Times*, and *Boston Globe*. He is a frequent commentator on CNN, Fox News, PBS, NPR, CSPAN and the Voice of America. His 17 books range from *Ronald Reagan: A Political Biography*, written in 1967, to *To Preserve and Protect: The Life of Edwin Meese III*, written in 2005, and also include *The Conservative Revolution: The Movement That Remade America* and *Educating for Liberty: The First Half Century of ISI*.

Educated at Duke University, the Sorbonne (Paris), and the Catholic University of America, Dr. Edwards was a fellow at the John F. Kennedy School of Government at Harvard University and is now an adjunct professor of politics at the Catholic University of America. He was founding director of the Institute on Political Journalism at Georgetown University, is the former president of the Philadelphia Society, and is cur-

rently chairman of the Victims of Communism Memorial
Foundation.

BOOKS LISTED BY TITLE

Books Listed by Title

BOOKS LISTED BY AUTHOR

Books Listed by Author

Books Listed by Author